The
MINISTRY GIFTS

Kenneth E. Hagin

Unless otherwise indicated, all Scripture quotations are taken from the *King James Version* of the Bible.

14 13 12 11 10 09 08   14 13 12 11 10 9 8

The Ministry Gifts
ISBN-13: 978-0-89276-073-2
ISBN-10: 0-89276-073-7

In the U.S. write:
Kenneth Hagin Ministries
P.O. Box 50126
Tulsa, OK 74150-0126
1-888-28-FAITH
www.rhema.org

In Canada write:
Kenneth Hagin Ministries
P.O. Box 335, Station D
Etobicoke (Toronto), Ontario
Canada, M9A 4X3
1-866-70-RHEMA
www.rhemacanada.org

Contents

Christ's Provision
For His Church

A. *He gave.* The Lord Jesus Christ gave these ministry gifts.

> **EPHESIANS 4:11**
> 11 And HE GAVE some, apostles; and some, prophets; and some, evangelists; and some, pastors and teachers.

B. *When did He give them?* When He ascended on High taking with Him the Old Testament saints who since their physical death had awaited in Paradise (Abraham's bosom) the consummation of God's great plan of redemption.

> **EPHESIANS 4:8-10**
> 8 Wherefore he saith, WHEN HE ASCENDED UP ON HIGH, he led captivity captive, and gave gifts unto men.
> 9 (Now that he ascended, what is it but that he also descended first into the lower parts of the earth?
> 10 He that descended is the same also that ascended up far above all heavens, that he might fill all things.)

C. *From where did He give ministry gifts?* These ministry gifts came (and come) from the Lord Jesus Christ Himself when He ascended and sat down on the right hand of the Majesty on High.

D. *For what purpose did He give these ministry gifts?*

> **EPHESIANS 4:12**
> **12 For the perfecting of the saints, for the work of the ministry, for the edifying of the body of Christ.**

1. *For the perfecting of the saints.*
   The Greek word (KATARTISMOS) translated "perfecting," according to W. E. *Vine's Expository Dictionary of New Testament Words,* denotes a fitting or preparing fully, implying a process leading to consummation.

   If one purpose for which the ministry gifts are given is the perfecting of the saints, will they ever reach maturity without them? No.

2. *For the work of the ministry.*

3. *For the edifying of the Body of Christ.*

E. *For how long did the Lord Jesus Christ give the ministry gifts?*

> **EPHESIANS 4:13**
> **13 TILL WE ALL COME in the unity of the faith, and of the knowledge of the Son of God, UNTO A PERFECT MAN, UNTO THE MEASURE OF THE STATURE OF THE FULNESS OF CHRIST.**

The ministry gifts are Christ's provision to the Church to build up, edify, and mature the saints.

An erroneous teaching which surfaced some time ago stressed what it termed "body ministry." (And there is a certain truth to that. God does use everyone.) But some taught, "We don't need pastors and ministers any longer. God is not using ministers anymore. God has a different program now."

The Scripture says that He gave these gifts to men, *"TILL WE ALL COME . . . unto a perfect man, unto the measure of the stature of the fulness of Christ."*

Until Jesus comes, "all of us" as a body of believers will never come to that place of maturity. When Jesus comes, some spiritual babies will just have been born into the family of God. They will not have had time to mature.

These ministry gifts are God's program for the maturing of the saints until Christ comes for His own.

F. *What is the ultimate aim in all ministry?*

> **EPHESIANS 4:13-16**
> **13 TILL WE ALL COME in the unity of the faith, and of the knowledge of the Son of God, UNTO A PERFECT MAN, UNTO THE MEASURE OF THE STATURE OF THE FULNESS OF CHRIST:**
> **14 THAT WE HENCEFORTH BE NO MORE CHILDREN, tossed to and fro, and carried about with every wind of doctrine, by the sleight of men, and cunning craftiness, whereby they lie in wait to deceive;**
> **15 But speaking the truth in love, MAY GROW UP INTO HIM in all things, which is the head, even Christ:**
> **16 From whom the whole body fitly joined together and compacted by that which every joint supplieth, according to the effectual working in the measure of every part, maketh increase of the body unto the edifying of itself in love.**

1. We need all five ministry gifts working together to bring the Body of Christ unto full stature in Christ.

2. Spiritual children are easily disturbed and swept about by false things.

3. The ministry gifts Christ placed in the Church help us *grow up into His image.*

3

4. We cannot reach that place without the function of the fivefold ministry.

5. Some areas of Christendom have not matured beyond a certain stage of growth because they recognize only two or three ministry gifts: evangelist and pastor, and sometimes teacher.

Summary: The ultimate aim of all ministry is not for self glory or to magnify the human in any way. It is entirely to edify and mature the Body of Christ. It takes all these ministries functioning together to edify — build up — the Body of Christ.

The Divine Call

A. *God hath set some in the Church. There is a divine call.*

> **1 CORINTHIANS 12:27,28**
> **27 Now ye are the body of Christ, and members in particular.**
> **28 AND GOD HATH SET SOME IN THE CHURCH, first apostles, secondarily prophets, thirdly teachers, after that miracles, then gifts of healings, helps, governments, diversities of tongues.**

1. Ephesians 4:11 says "Jesus gave." This passage says "God set."

2. Notice this Corinthian passage calls the Body of Christ the Church. The Church is the Body of Christ. The Body of Christ is the Church.

B. God sets ministry gifts in the Church — *not man.*

1. There is a vast difference between God setting some in the Church — and man setting some in the Church.

2. A study of Church history reveals that down through the centuries, various groups have endeavored to get back to what they

call New Testament practices.

They've set up organizations which often were something man manufactured — something in the flesh; something carnal.

They "called" and "set" people who had no divine calling into certain offices.

This is unscriptural.

God does the setting.
God does the calling.

C. You do not enter the ministry — any phase of it — just because *you* feel it is a holy calling and you'd like to respond.

  1. You cannot make yourself a ministry gift.

  2. It is dangerous to do something just because *you* want to do it.

D. You do not enter the ministry because *someone else* tells you that you are suited for it.

  Personal experience: When I was a pastor, I watched young people in the church who were apt to work for God. Some of them, I believe, were called. Some of them, I am certain, were not. I have seen other members in the church ruin some of these young people by getting around them and saying, "I believe you are called to preach," and so forth. They tried to do it and failed. Oftentimes they got out of church completely because of it.

  1. Don't go into the ministry because somebody else called you.

  2. Don't go into the ministry because your mother called you.

  3. Don't go into the ministry because your father called you.

  4. Husbands, if you are a minister of the gospel and have a divine

call on your life, don't try to call your wife into the ministry. Let her be the helper who is meet (or proper) for you, as God designed her to be. Include her in every way you possibly can.

5. Wives, if you are called, don't try to make a preacher out of your husband if he is not one. But don't shut him out of your life. Work him into your life, and even your ministry, in every way you possibly can.

6. There is a divine call to the ministry. You must determine whether or not it is on your life. Don't try to go into the ministry without a calling from God to do so.

E. *How can you tell a divine call?*

1. You will have the conviction in your own spirit.
   You will have the witness in your own heart.
   You will have the spiritual equipment — gifts of the Spirit — that go along with the office or offices to which you are called.

Personal experience: I just knew I was called deep down inside myself. How? By an inward intuition. It was always with me. It was as much a part of me on the inside as my ears were a part of me on the outside.

2. God deals with man's spirit.

3. Learn to listen to your spirit.

   a. Learn to listen down on the inside of you and you will know many things you don't otherwise know.

   b. But if you are just messing along in the world, about half-dedicated, half-in and half-out because you are living too much in the carnal realm, carnality will dominate you, and you won't be conscious of your spirit.

   c. If you are fully dedicated and consecrated to God to do anything He wants you to do, you will become conscious of that something inside you.

    d.   There will be a divine compulsion on the inside of you.

F.   The methods by which men are called are unimportant. But obedience to the call is important.

    1.   If methods were important, the Bible would emphasize them; it does not.

    2.   The Bible has much to say about obedience.

    3.   Sometimes God does move in extraordinary ways. But this is not the rule.

        a.   *Visions.* Sometimes people will have visions. Paul did. I have had visions. But I was in the ministry 15 years before I did. I went into the ministry without any kind of "supernatural" (if you want to call it that — actually, everything of God is *supernatural*) visitation. I went just by the inward intuition; the inward witness.

        b.   *Prophecy.* Ministry gifts *are not* set in the Church by prophecy. However, a confirmation to the ministry may come through prophecy.

ACTS 13:1,2
1 Now there were in the church which was at Antioch certain prophets and teachers; as Barnabas, and Simeon ... and Lucius ... and Manaen ... and Saul.
2 As they ministered to the Lord, and fasted, the Holy Ghost said, Separate me Barnabas and Saul for the work whereunto I HAVE CALLED THEM.

Barnabas and Saul were not called by prophecy. They were not set in the ministry by prophecy or by man. God just confirmed their call through prophecy.

Personal experience: In the last church I pastored, we were all praying around the altar one night in united prayer. I was laying hands on various ones and praying over them as the Spirit of God seemed to lead me.

Suddenly, I was drawn like a magnet to a very quiet young lady who was actually timid in a sense. When I laid hands on her head to pray, I was surprised to find myself saying, "This is the confirmation of what I said to you at 3 o'clock this afternoon as you were praying in the storm cellar. I told you I would confirm it."

I didn't know what that meant. And I didn't ask her about it right then because she began to cry and pray even more.

I telephoned her later and asked, "Did that mean anything to you? Were you in the cellar praying at 3 o'clock?"

"Yes," she said, "the Lord said that He called me to the ministry and that He would confirm it in the service tonight."

Notice she was not set in the Church as a ministry gift by prophecy. It was confirmed that way — but she wasn't set into the ministry that way.

1. If a so-called prophecy does not confirm what you have in your own spirit, forget it.

Personal experience: A man once told me that a "prophet" had laid hands on him and had given him five spiritual gifts, including gifts of healings and the word of knowledge.

This so-called prophet had said to him, "I've been observing you, and I've noticed that the word of knowledge and gifts of healings operate in you."

This man said to me, I must have these gifts because that prophet said I did. Maybe you can tell me how to operate them."

I said, "In all these months since the man laid hands on you, have these spiritual gifts ever manifested in your life?"

"No," he said.

I said, "If I were you, I would just forget it. In the first place, that so-called prophet didn't give you anything. Only

God can give spiritual gifts. In the second place, if spiritual gifts were there, they would endeavor to come into manifestation. You would have some kind of intuition about it. If I were you, I would just stay in the church here and be faithful."

I was preaching in the area some time later. I noticed he had remained a layman, faithful to God and was a blessing to the church. Had he tried to enter some other office, he could have become a curse to that church, instead of a blessing.

G.   Seeing a *need* is not a *call* to the ministry.

1.   If we are not careful, we slip into the attitude of the Church in general that seeing a need is a call. This is not scriptural. *There is a divine call, given by God alone.*

2.   Naturally, as Christians, anytime we see a need, we are concerned about that need and will endeavor with all the ability we have to minister to that need. That is scripturally correct. But it is not to be confused with the divine call to the ministry.

H.   An anointing evidences a divine call.

Personal experience: Many years ago I heard a man preach at a great convention of 5,000 people or more. "Seeing a need is a call," he stated. Although he was in the ministry, he said, "If I have ever been called to the ministry, I don't know it."

I thought to myself, *If he hadn't told us, all of us would have known it in 15 minutes anyway.* There was no anointing on him.

When a person is called to the ministry, there is an anointing that just comes upon him or her to stand in an office. Otherwise the person would just stand up and talk. It's good to talk and share whatever you have, but that's different from being called to a ministry and being set in the Church.

I.   If God didn't call you to full-time ministry, don't try to get into it; you will be a misfit.

J.   Knowing that you *know* you are divinely called settles the matter once and for all. There should be no confusion on the subject.

Personal experience: As I said, I entered the ministry without any kind of supernatural visitation. I just went by the inward intuition — the inward witness. And I have never been confused on the subject.

Yet through the years, especially during the 12 years I pastored, I've seen many ministers who were up and down, even wondering whether or not they were really called.

And I can tell you why they were. It was because they were living by flesh and in the mental realm instead of in the spiritual realm.

If Sunday School was down, they were down. Their faces were long. If finances were down, they were down.

You'd hear them talk like this: "I don't know whether God called me to preach or not anyway. If I can ever get the Sunday School back up where it was . . ." "If I can get the finances back where they were . . ." "I think I'll just leave."

Some of them asked me, "Brother Hagin, don't you ever get down?"

I said, "No, I stay up all the time. If we just have a half a crowd, I'm up just as much as when we have a big crowd. You see, I know God called me. And I know He called me to come here. So I will stay until He tells me to leave. If no one shows up but two snaggle-toothed old women, I'll give them my best and stay faithful.

"I never even think about, *I might be out of the will of God.* Because I know God said, 'Go.' He's an intelligent Being. I'm an intelligent being. He will communicate with me and tell me when to leave."

You see, you can worry and bother yourself and open the door for the devil to have a field day in you.

This was my motto before I ever read that Wigglesworth said it. I guess any person of faith would say it.

I am not moved by what I see.
I am not moved by what I feel.
I am moved only by what I believe.

Learn that spiritual things are more real than natural things.
Learn to look to your spirit.
Your spirit will tell you.
Your spirit knows things your head doesn't know.

preach and to teach the Word is always right.) Eventually —
when you reach some maturity, both mentally and spiritually — God will let you know what your calling is.

5. Take time to wait on God. Take time to fast and pray. Take time
to find His perfect will for your life and ministry.

    a.   I shall never forget the day I was kneeling at the altar in my
church when I said to the Lord, "Lord, I've been waiting on
You for 10 years."

Just as plain as some man talking to me, He said, "No, you
haven't. I've been waiting on you for 10 years. I've been waiting on you to make up your mind to obey me. I've been waiting on you to make up your mind to do what I want you to
do."

    b.   In the first vision when Jesus appeared to me, He said,
"When you left your last church you entered into the first
phase of your ministry."

I was shocked. I'd been in the ministry 15 years. I said,
"Lord, I spent 15 years in the ministry, and You blessed me."

He said, "Certainly. I blessed you all I could. I blessed the
Word you preached because I honor My Word. That doesn't
mean I was honoring you."

Then He said this, *"Many ministers live and die and never
get into the first phase of the ministry I have for them. That's
the reason many of them die prematurely."*

(You see, if you are not in the perfect will of God, you are in
a place where Satan can attack you. If you are not in the perfect will of God, it is difficult to claim the highest that
belongs to you.)

"Many ministers live and die and never get into the first phase of the ministry I have for them." I thought about it through the years. I could have done the same thing.

"Oh, yes," somebody said, "the Lord singled you out, though."

No, He never did a thing until I started seeking Him. He never moved. He never told me a thing.

c. *Stay open to God.*

If you settle down into another call, or another area of ministry and don't keep the communication lines open between you and Heaven, God will let you go on and suffer the consequences of being out of the perfect will of God.

d. When you're only in the *permissive will* of God, something won't seem right to you. You can tell the difference. It's sort of like washing your feet with your socks on.

G. *Do not intrude into the wrong office.*

1. I think the thing that hinders people in the ministry more than anything else is trying to stand in the wrong office. The tragedy is that people live and die there and never know it.

2. *It can cost you your ministry.*

a. Charles Finney was the greatest soulwinner and evangelist since the New Testament days. When he was about 80, he wrote, "I know many things, deeper things of God, than I am able to teach. If I do teach these things, I lose the ability to win souls."

Why, if he knew these things, couldn't he teach them? (Of course he could share them with others individually, but he didn't teach them to the Church at large.) Because that was not his calling. Let the teachers do that. His calling was the evangelistic office. His calling was to win souls. If he got over into the wrong office, he ceased to be a blessing.

    b.   Part of my calling is to be a teacher. I get more people saved by teaching than I ever did by preaching evangelistic sermons because that is what God told me to do.

3.   Intruding into the wrong office *can cost you your life.*

    a.   Holy things are holy. In the Old Testament if someone besides the High Priest intruded into the Holy of Holies, he fell dead instantly. He had intruded into the wrong office.

    b.   It is dangerous to play with holy things.

    c.   The calling of God is holy.

    d.   The ministry of God is holy.

H.   *Develop Character.*

1.   More is required of people who are separated unto an office.

2.   Set the right example always.

3.   Provide things honest in the sight of all men.

4.   Fill your place with dignity.

If you are called of God to stand in an office, that office demands respect. If you have respect for the office you are in, you will teach people to have respect for that office.

Variety and Balance

A. One of the most fascinating things concerning the ministry gifts of Christ is their variety.

   1. *Apostles.* The apostle's office seems to embrace almost every type of ministry.

   2. *Prophets.* The prophet's ministry is inspirational. He speaks by direct, divine inspiration and revelation.

   3. *Evangelists.* The evangelist has a direct endowment from the Lord to PREACH the Word for the salvation of souls.

   4. *Pastors.* Pastors are the shepherds of God's sheep.

   5. *Teachers.* Those who fill the office of teacher teach the Word, not by natural ability, but by the divine ability of the Holy Spirit.

B. These ministry gifts have been given to the Church to bring a balance in the Church.

   1. We see an example of ministry gifts working together in the church at Antioch (Acts 13:1).

2. The matter of a balance of ministry gifts in the Body of Christ is vitally important to be effective.

3. One ministry gift office alone cannot hope to effectively be able to minister to all the needs of the entire Body of Christ.

4. At the extreme are those who think a minister doesn't have a valid ministry unless he ministers mostly by manifestations of the gifts of the Spirit, rather than by teaching or preaching the Word.

C. The Body of Christ needs to realize that Christ gave a diversity of ministry gifts to the Church for a reason. All of them are essential in order for the Church of the Lord Jesus Christ to come unto full stature in Christ.

1. Teachers can sometimes think evangelists are too flamboyant and sensational.

2. Evangelists can think teachers are dry and dogmatic.

3. Evangelists and teachers often agree saying that prophets can sometimes be intense and extreme.

4. All such attitudes are wrong.

5. There can be extremes in all usage of ministry gifts. Yet we must not repress the gift of God, for we may quench the Spirit of God.

D. It is God's divine plan that each ministry gift provide a check and balance to correct and complement the other.

1. The prophet is to inspire the teacher.

2. The teacher is to steady the prophet.

3. The evangelist is to continually remind us of the lost and dying world and its need for the Gospel.

4. The pastor is to demonstrate to us that souls still need much nurturing and care after they have been won to the Lord.

5. And the apostle, above all, is to inspire and lead the way for gaining ground by establishing new works for the Lord.

E. The ultimate goal of all ministry is to unite — not divide.

Ephesians 4:13 reads, "Till we all come in the unity," and not, "Till we are all divided into splinter groups."

F. A person can stand in more than one office; we separate ministry offices to define them.

The Apostle

1 CORINTHIANS 12:28
28 And God hath set some in the church, FIRST APOSTLES,
secondarily prophets, thirdly teachers, after that miracles, then
gifts of healings, helps, governments, diversities of tongues.

EPHESIANS 4:11
11 And he gave some, APOSTLES. . . .

A.   The ministry gift which heads the list is the apostle. However, that does
not mean it is the most important ministry gift in the local body today,
nor does it mean that apostles are to dominate over other ministry gifts
in the Body of Christ. In other words, Paul was not establishing a hier-
archy for local church government by the way he listed the ministry
gifts here.

1.   Actually, Paul was probably listing these offices in the order he
did because of the way God "set" or *developed* ministry gifts in the
Early Church.

2.   You see, in the establishing of the *universal Church* following the
resurrection of Jesus, the apostles and prophets were obviously
the most important ministry offices because they were the first
ministry gifts to be developed or "set" in the Body of Christ.

a. Also, they were foundational apostles and prophets — they laid the foundation for the New Testament.

b. In other words, they were initially the most important offices when the Early Church was just beginning because they brought forth the revelation of the New Testament, which is the foundation upon which the Church in all generations is to be established.

3. However, in terms of the operation of the *local church* today, First Corinthians 12:28 is not a list of the offices of apostles and prophets in their order of importance. Neither is it a list indicating that apostles and prophets are the *governing* offices within the *local* church.

a. Apostles and prophets do not make up the office of "governments" found in First Corinthians 12:28. For one thing, Paul listed "governments" as an entirely separate office. It probably refers to the pastoral office.

b. For another thing, some offices are listed in a certain order in the ministry list in Ephesians 4:11, and in another order in the ministry list of First Corinthians 12:28.

c. Therefore, this list in First Corinthians 12:28 does not indicate that the offices of the apostle and prophet are the most important or the governing offices in the *local* church today.

B. The most significant statement of fact in the Bible regarding this office is that it was *filled by Christ Himself*.

HEBREWS 3:1
1 Wherefore, holy brethren, partakers of the heavenly calling, consider the Apostle and High Priest of our profession, Christ Jesus.

C. The Greek word APOSTOLOS translated apostle means *one sent forth, a sent one*.

D. *Jesus Christ is the greatest example of a sent one.*

> **JOHN 20:21**
> **21 Then said Jesus to them again, Peace be unto you: AS MY FATHER HATH SENT ME, even so send I you.**

E. A true apostle is always *one with a commission* — not one who merely goes, but one who is sent by the Holy Spirit.

1. Acts 13 gives a picture of the sending forth of Barnabas and Paul to be apostles to the Gentiles.

F. *The signs of an apostle.* The Bible speaks of the signs of an apostle:

> **2 CORINTHIANS 12:12**
> **12 Truly THE SIGNS of an apostle were wrought among you in all patience, in SIGNS, and WONDERS, and MIGHTY DEEDS.**

What are these signs?
Signs, wonders, and mighty deeds.

G. *The fruit of an apostle.* The Bible also talks about the works or fruit of the apostolic ministry:

> **1 CORINTHIANS 9:1**
> **1 Am I not an apostle? am I not free? have I not seen Jesus Christ our Lord? are not ye MY WORK in the Lord?**

1. In defending his apostleship, Paul could rightly say, *". . . are not ye my work in the Lord?"* The fruit of Paul's apostolic ministry were *people* who were solidly established in the *Word*.

> **1 CORINTHIANS 9:2**
> **2 If I be not an apostle unto others, yet doubtless I am to you: for the seal of mine apostleship are ye in the Lord.**

2. Paul could also point to solidly established churches and say that they were the seal or the *fruit* of his apostolic ministry. In his epistle, Paul addresses many of his letters to those churches he had established. And in First Corinthians 4:15, we see the true nature of the apostolic call.

> **1 CORINTHIANS 4:15**
> **15 For though ye have ten thousand instructors in Christ, YET HAVE YE NOT MANY FATHERS: for in Christ Jesus I have begotten you through the gospel.**

3. Paul was really a spiritual father to those whom he had established in the faith. Although Paul founded and established many churches, he didn't rule over those people, any more than a father dictatorially rules over his children whom he loves.

    a. Paul's apostolic office didn't give him the authority to tell people and churches what to do in every area of life. Yet some of the so-called "apostles" today try to run every aspect of the local church, including people's personal lives.

    b. Notice Paul's statements to every church he wrote in the epistles. He didn't command them. He wasn't a dictator over them. He addressed them in fatherly tones of genuine care and concern: *"Now I Paul myself BESEECH you by the MEEKNESS and GENTLENESS of Christ . . ."* (2 Cor. 10:1).

    > **1 THESSALONIANS 2:6-12**
    > **6 Nor of men sought we glory, neither of you, nor yet of others, when we might have been burdensome, AS THE APOSTLES OF CHRIST.**
    > **7 But WE WERE GENTLE AMONG YOU, even as a NURSE CHERISHETH HER CHILDREN:**
    > **8 So being AFFECTIONATELY DESIROUS of you, we were willing to have imparted unto you, not the gospel of God only, but also our own souls, because YE WERE DEAR UNTO US.**

9 For ye remember, brethren, OUR LABOUR and TRAVAIL: for labouring night and day, because we would not be chargeable unto any of you, WE PREACHED UNTO YOU THE GOSPEL OF GOD.
10 Ye are witnesses, and God also, how HOLILY and JUSTLY and UNBLAMEABLY WE BEHAVED OURSELVES AMONG YOU that believe:
11 As ye know how we EXHORTED and COMFORTED and CHARGED every one of you, AS A FATHER DOTH HIS CHILDREN,
12 THAT YE WOULD WALK WORTHY OF GOD, who hath called you unto his kingdom and glory.

c. Paul demonstrated his attitude in these passages of Scripture. It is not an attitude of trying to lord it over people and rule them. What did Paul *exhort, comfort,* and *charge* believers?

d. Did Paul demand his right to dominate them? Assuredly not! Did he command all churches under his "authority" to tithe to him as some so-called "apostles" today are doing? A thousand times, no! He exhorted and charged believers *to walk worthy of God.*

e. Paul's apostolic care and concern for the churches is made even more clear in *The Amplified Bible.*

1 THESSALONIANS 2:7,11 *(Amplified)*
7 But we behaved gently when we were among you, LIKE A DEVOTED MOTHER NURSING AND CHERISHING HER OWN CHILDREN. . . .
11 . . . like a FATHER [DEALING WITH HIS CHILDREN], we used to exhort each of you personally, stimulating and encouraging and charging you.

f. There is a vast difference between Paul's attitude demonstrated in his letters to the churches, and the attitude of some so-called "apostles" today who are dominating people and trying to rule over them harshly in pride and superiority.

g. Some of these so-called "apostles" today, command people by saying, "You have to listen to me and do what I say because I'm an apostle." That's not scriptural. A statement like that can't be proved by the Bible.

H. *Characteristics of an apostle.* An apostle is first and foremost a preacher or a teacher, or a preacher and a teacher of the Word.

1 TIMOTHY 2:7
7 Whereunto I am ordained a PREACHER, and an APOSTLE, (I speak the truth in Christ, and lie not;) a TEACHER of the Gentiles in faith and verity.

2 TIMOTHY 1:11
11 Whereunto I am appointed a PREACHER, and an APOSTLE, and a TEACHER of the Gentiles.

1. Notice Paul didn't say, "I am first ordained an apostle." No, Paul said he was first ordained a preacher because he was first and foremost a preacher and a teacher of the Word of God.

I. To stand in this office, one must have a deep personal encounter with the Lord and an ongoing spiritually strong relationship with Him and His Word — something beyond the ordinary.

1. *Paul.* Notice something Paul said in defending his apostleship: *"Am I not an apostle? am I not free? HAVE I NOT SEEN JESUS CHRIST OUR LORD? . . ."* (1 Cor. 9:1). Paul did not see Jesus in the flesh as the twelve did. But he saw Jesus in a spiritual vision (Acts 9:3-6). Paul had a deep spiritual experience with the Lord. Even his conversion was beyond the ordinary.

Paul had such a deep spiritual experience with the Lord that he could say concerning what he knew about the Lord's Supper, *"For I have received of the Lord that which also I delivered unto you . . ."*

(1 Cor. 11:23). Paul didn't learn what he knew about this subject from the other apostles. He got it by revelation. Jesus gave it to him.

2. Paul wasn't taught the Gospel he preached by man. The Spirit of God taught it to him. *"But I certify you, brethren, that the gospel which was preached of me is not after man. For I neither received it of man, neither was I taught it, but by the revelation of Jesus Christ"* (Gal. 1:11,12). We have heard others teach these Bible truths, but Paul had not. Look at the rest of this passage in Galatians concerning Paul's revelation — proof of his deep experience with the Lord.

> **GALATIANS 1:13-17**
> **13 For ye have heard of my conversation in time past in the Jews' religion, how that beyond measure I persecuted the church of God, and wasted it:**
> **14 And profited in the Jews' religion above many my equals in mine own nation, being more exceedingly zealous of the traditions of my fathers.**
> **15 But when it pleased God, who separated me from my mother's womb, and called me by his grace,**
> **16 To reveal his Son in me, that I might preach him among the heathen; IMMEDIATELY I CONFERRED NOT WITH FLESH AND BLOOD:**
> **17 NEITHER WENT I UP TO JERUSALEM TO THEM WHICH WERE APOSTLES BEFORE ME; BUT I WENT INTO ARABIA, AND RETURNED AGAIN UNTO DAMASCUS.**

How long was Paul in Arabia? No one knows. But it was while he was in Arabia that Paul received the revelation of the Gospel of which he writes in every epistle.

> **GALATIANS 1:18,19,21-24**
> **18 THEN AFTER THREE YEARS I WENT UP TO JERUSALEM TO SEE PETER, AND ABODE WITH HIM FIFTEEN DAYS.**

19 But other of the apostles saw I none, save James the Lord's brother. . . .
21 Afterwards I came into the regions of Syria and Cilicia;
22 And was unknown by face unto the churches of Judaea which were in Christ:
23 But they had heard only, That he which persecuted us in times past now preacheth the faith which once he destroyed.
24 And they glorified God in me.

Three years after Paul *returned* from Damascus, he went to Jerusalem and spent two weeks with Peter.

GALATIANS 2:1,2
1 THEN FOURTEEN YEARS AFTER I WENT UP AGAIN TO JERUSALEM with Barnabas, and took Titus with me also.
2 AND I WENT UP BY REVELATION, and communicated unto them that gospel which I preach among the Gentiles, but privately to them which were of reputation, lest by any means I should run, or had run, in vain.

Paul had been preaching for 17 years by then. He didn't know what the apostles preached. He hadn't heard them. He'd been with Peter only a brief two-week period. After which he preached 14 more years before the Spirit of God revealed to him that he should go up to Jerusalem and communicate with these brethren.

Paul did indeed have a deep religious experience with the Lord Jesus Christ!

J. *An apostle's ministry seems to embrace all other ministry gifts.* The distinguishing result is *the ability to establish churches.*

1. The apostle has some workings of all five offices, which would include the pastoral equipment of governments. (Weymouth translates the word "governments" as *powers of organization.*)

2. After churches are established, apostles may exercise oversight over those churches they have established themselves (1 Cor. 9:1,2) until those churches are adequately established with spiritual authority of their own.

   Comments: There are many who call themselves apostles who want to dominate and rule people. They say, "I'm an apostle. I have authority. You have to do what I say." In New Testament days the apostles only exercised oversight over the churches they established themselves. Paul never exercised any authority over the church at Jerusalem, nor any of the churches that other apostles had established.

   Remember, these offices are in power and not in name only. If the power is not there to establish churches, then a person is not an apostle in the full sphere of the office.

3. A *missionary* who is really called of God and sent by the Holy Ghost is an apostle.

   a. Acts 13:2,4. The Holy Spirit said, "*. . . Separate me Barnabas and Saul for the work whereunto I have called them.*" Then verse 4 says, "*So they, being SENT FORTH by the Holy Ghost, departed. . . .*"

      Barnabas and Saul were "sent ones." They left on their first missionary journey to the Gentiles.

   b. The New Testament never mentions missionaries, yet it is an important office. It is here in the office of an apostle.

   c. The missionary will have the ability of all the ministry gifts.

1. He will do the work of the evangelist.
   He will get people saved.
2. He will do the work of the teacher.
   He will teach and establish people.

3. He will do the work of the pastor.
   He will pastor and shepherd people for a while.

   a. In studying closely the life of the Apostle Paul, we note that he said he never built on a foundation someone else had laid. He endeavored to preach the gospel where Christ was not named (Rom. 15:20).

   He always stayed in a place from six months to three years.

   b. His real calling was not to be a pastor, but he stayed long enough to get believers established in the truth, and then moved on.

K. *Are there apostles today?*

1. Four classes of apostles.

The Lord said to me in a visitation which took place in July 1987 that there were four classes of apostles and that each class of apostle had a different anointing. After I studied it out in the Word of God, I could see this truth for myself.

a. *Jesus the Chief Apostle:* Jesus Himself is the Chief Apostle and stands in a class by Himself. We find in Hebrews 3:1 that Jesus is called the Apostle and High Priest of our profession.

He was a "Sent One" from the Father to make atonement for the sins of the world. No other apostle (or sent one) will ever have that calling.

b. *Apostles of the Lamb:* These were the twelve apostles who were eyewitnesses of Jesus' life, ministry, death, burial, and resurrection (Acts 1:21,22). This was their purpose — to witness Jesus' earthly ministry and to give testimony of His ministry to the world. No one, not even Paul, could be an apostle in the sense the original twelve were. There are only twelve Apostles of the Lamb (Rev. 21:14).

The Bible gives the qualifications for the original twelve Apostles of the Lamb when they were to select one to take Judas' place.

ACTS 1:15-22

15 And in those days Peter stood up in the midst of the disciples, and said, (the number of names together were about an hundred and twenty,)

16 Men and brethren, this scripture must needs have been fulfilled, which the Holy Ghost by the mouth of David spake before concerning Judas, which was guide to them that took Jesus.

17 For he was numbered with us, and had obtained part of this ministry.

18 Now this man purchased a field with the reward of iniquity; and falling headlong, he burst asunder in the midst, and all his bowels gushed out.

19 And it was known unto all the dwellers at Jerusalem; insomuch as that field is called in their proper tongue, Aceldama, that is to say, The field of blood.

20 For it is written in the book of Psalms, Let his habitation be desolate, and let no man dwell therein: and his bishoprick let another take.

21 Wherefore of these men WHICH HAVE COMPANIED WITH US ALL THE TIME THAT THE LORD JESUS WENT IN AND OUT AMONG US,

22 BEGINNING FROM THE BAPTISM OF JOHN, UNTO THAT SAME DAY THAT HE WAS TAKEN UP FROM US, MUST ONE BE ORDAINED TO BE A WITNESS WITH US OF HIS RESURRECTION.

To be one of the twelve Apostles of the Lamb, one had to have accompanied them — the apostles and Jesus — all the time Jesus went in and out among them for the three and a half years of His ministry. Paul was not with them.

The original twelve were sent ones to be eye witnesses of the ministry, the works, the life, death, burial, resurrection, and ascension of the Lord Jesus Christ. They stood in a place no other apostles or ministries can ever stand.

c. *New Testament Apostles:* This includes Paul, Barnabas, and the other apostles of the New Testament. In addition to calling Jesus Christ an Apostle, and the twelve Apostles of the Lamb, the New Testament calls several others apostles:

1. *Barnabas and Paul* (Acts 14:14).

2. *James the Lord's brother* (Gal. 1:19).

3. *Andronicus and Junia* (Rom. 16:7).

4. *Silvanus and Timotheus* (1 Thess. 1:1; 2:6).

5. *Apollos* (1 Cor. 4:4-9).

6. *Two unnamed brethren* (2 Cor. 8:23).*

7. *Epaphroditus* (Phil. 2:25).*

*The word translated "messenger" in these verses is the same Greek word translated "apostle" elsewhere. It can also mean a *representative* or a *delegate.*

The New Testament apostles were not apostles in the same sense that the twelve Apostles of the Lamb were. For one reason, they were not eyewitnesses of Jesus' life and ministry. Second, they seemed to have more limited callings. Paul, for example, was an apostle (a sent one) to the Gentiles only (*see* 2 Tim. 1:11).

There is much talk today about the need for modern-day apostles to lay the foundation for the Church. But the foundation of the Church Universal has already been laid! This work was done by the Apostles of the Lamb and the other apostles of the New Testament.

Paul explains this in First Corinthians 3:10:

1 CORINTHIANS 3:10
10 According to the grace of God which is given unto me, as a wise masterbuilder, I HAVE LAID THE FOUNDATION, and another buildeth thereon. But let every man take heed how he buildeth thereupon.

EPHESIANS 2:20
20 And are built upon THE FOUNDATION OF THE APOSTLES and prophets, Jesus Christ Himself being the chief corner stone.

The Apostles of the Lamb and the other New Testament apostles laid the foundation of the Church by giving testimony of Jesus' earthly mission, by being the earliest pioneers and preachers of the gospel, and by receiving the Word of God and recording it in written form in what we now know as the New Testament. Modern-day apostles are not called to lay the foundation of the Church. They have an entirely different calling and mission.

d. *Apostles of Today:* There are no apostles today in the three classes listed above. There are no foundation-laying apostles today. If the foundation was not laid by the apostles of the New Testament and we need modern-day apostles to do it, then we need a new cornerstone as well. Of course, that is foolish. The work of the apostle today is to found and establish individual local churches throughout the world; to go into new territory and pioneer churches where there are no churches just as I've mentioned previously.

2. Many question whether or not the office of the apostle even exists today. *But thank God, it does.* Let's go back to Ephesians 4.

> **EPHESIANS 4:8,11-13**
> **8 Wherefore he saith, When he ascended up on high, he led captivity captive, and gave gifts unto men. . . .**
> **11 And he gave some, apostles; and some, prophets; and some, evangelists; and some, pastors and teachers;**
> **12 For the perfecting of the saints, for the work of the ministry, for the edifying of the body of Christ:**
> **13 Till we all come in the unity of the faith, and of the knowledge of the Son of God, unto a perfect man, unto the measure of the stature of the fulness of Christ.**

a. If God has taken any of these ministries out of the list, the Bible should have told us that He gave them for just a little while.

b. *ALL* of these ministry gifts were given for the perfecting of the saints, for the work of the ministry, for the edifying of the Body of Christ. This includes apostles.

c. For how long did He give them? All of them were given *"Till we all come in the unity of the faith, and of the knowledge of the Son of God, unto a perfect man, unto the measure of the stature of the fulness of Christ"* (Eph. 4:13).

L. *What marks do we look for in an apostle today?*

1. First and foremost a preacher or a teacher of the Word.

2. Outstanding spiritual gifts.

3. Deep personal experience.

4. Power and ability to establish churches.

5. Able to provide adequate spiritual leadership.

Comments: If God did call you to be an apostle, I wouldn't bother about it. Acts 13:1 reads, *"Now there were in the church that was at Antioch certain prophets and teachers; as Barnabas, and Simeon . . . and Lucius . . . and Manaen . . . and Saul."* Each of these men was either a prophet, or a teacher, and or a prophet and a teacher (one can stand in more than one office). So we know from study of the Scriptures that Paul was both a prophet and a teacher. Acts 14:14 calls him an apostle. He became an apostle when *God* set him in that office.

Remember this: Don't get taken up with names and titles. If I didn't know what God called me to, I wouldn't bother a minute about it.

If I sensed the call on the inside of me, I would just prepare myself in the Word and preach and teach, and then let God eventually set me in the office He has for me.

Barnabas and Paul were not set in the office of apostle to begin with, but God eventually did set them there.

And also remember this: God rewards faithfulness. He doesn't reward offices.

A prophet won't receive any more reward in that day than a janitor who was faithful in his ministry of helps.

Higher offices do not receive any more reward; there is just a greater responsibility.

God rewards faithfulness!

The Prophet

Introduction: In February 1959, the Lord Jesus Christ appeared to me and spoke to me one and a half hours about the ministry of a prophet. That vision is told in some detail in my book, *I Believe in Visions*. Much of the information contained in this syllabus was revealed to me at that time. The Lord also appeared to me in 1987 and spoke to me about the ministry gifts, notably the offices of the apostle and prophet.

> **1 CORINTHIANS 12:28**
> **28 And God hath set some in the church, first apostles, SECONDARILY PROPHETS. . . .**

> **EPHESIANS 4:11**
> **11 And he gave some, apostles; and some, PROPHETS. . . .**

A.   *Are there prophets today?*

　　1.   Some would tell us that the office of the prophet has been done away with — that there were prophets in the Old Testament and in the New Testament, but there are none today.

　　　　a.   There is no scriptural evidence for this.

2. The Word of God tells us that He gave some apostles, some prophets, some evangelists, some pastors, and some teachers (Eph. 4:11).

   a. Some say the only ministries we have today are evangelists, pastors, and teachers.

   b. The Word of God makes no distinction. It seems to me the list either stands or falls together.

   c. For what purpose were they given? *"For the perfecting of the saints, for the work of the ministry, for the edifying of the body of Christ."*

   Have the saints all been perfected yet? Is there any work of the ministry going on today? Does the Body of Christ need edifying? Emphatically, yes! Then all these ministry gifts should be in operation.

   d. These ministry gifts will be necessary until Jesus comes for His Church.

B. *What constitutes the office of a prophet?*

   1. Commenting on what the New Testament Greek says concerning the prophet, an outstanding Greek scholar said, "He speaks from the impulse of a *sudden inspiration*, from the light of a sudden revelation at the moment. The idea of speaking from sudden revelation seems here to be fundamental, as relating either to future events, or the mind of the Spirit in general."

   A prophet speaks by direct divine inspiration, an immediate revelation — not something he thought of, but something given at the spur of the moment by sudden inspiration.

   2. To stand in the office of a prophet, *one is first of all a minister of the Gospel*, separated and called to the ministry with the calling of God upon his life. The prophet is a *ministry* gift.

a. A prophet is first of all a preacher or a teacher of the Word.

b. There are no prophets among what we call the laity — because a prophet is one who is called to the full-time ministry.

c. A layman may prophesy, but you are not a prophet just because you prophesy.

1. Paul encouraged *the entire church* at Corinth to covet to prophesy (1 Cor. 14:1).

   Then he gives the definition of what the simple gift of prophecy is: *"But he that prophesieth speaketh unto men to edification, and exhortation, and comfort"* (v. 3).

   Yet the answer to the question "Are all prophets?" is obviously "No" (1 Cor. 12:29).

2. *Distinguish between prophesying* — though a prophet might prophesy — *and the ministry of the prophet.*

   ACTS 21:8-11
   8 And the next day we that were of Paul's company departed, and came unto Caesarea: and we entered into the house of Philip the evangelist, which was one of the seven; and abode with him.
   9 And the same man had four daughters, virgins, WHICH DID PROPHESY.
   10 And as we tarried there many days, there came down from Judaea A CERTAIN PROPHET, named Agabus.
   11 And when he was come unto us, he took Paul's girdle, and bound his own hands and feet, and said, Thus saith the Holy Ghost, So shall the Jews at Jerusalem bind the man that owneth this girdle, and shall deliver him into the hands of the Gentiles.

The four daughters of Philip did prophesy. That means *they were operating in the simple gift of prophecy,* "speaking unto men to edification, and exhortation, and comfort" (1 Cor. 14:3).

Agabus was a prophet. And although a prophet may prophesy what is revealed at the moment, Agabus is not prophesying here. He is just telling what the Holy Spirit had previously revealed to him.

3.   *To stand in the office of prophet, one must have a more consistent manifestation of at least two of the revelation gifts* (word of wisdom, word of knowledge, or discerning of spirits) *plus prophecy.*

   a.   The three *revelation* gifts are:

      1.   *Word of wisdom:* Supernatural revelation by the Spirit of God concerning the divine purpose in the mind and will of God. Always speaks of the future.

      2.   *Word of knowledge:* Supernatural revelation by the Spirit of God of facts in the mind of God concerning people, places, or things. Always present or past tense.

      3.   *Discerning of spirits:* Supernatural insight into the realm of spirits. Seeing and hearing in the spirit realm.

   b.   Any Spirit-filled believer might have occasional manifestations of these gifts as the Spirit wills and as the need arises. But a prophet would also stand in the place of preacher or teacher of the Word and would have a more consistent manifestation of them. The difference is that the prophet has a ministry along this line. It becomes a ministry gift on a higher level.

   c.   A prophet is one who has visions and revelations.

   d.   *There are three types of revelations and three types of visions.* The highest type of revelation and the lowest type of vision are similar and sometimes a person cannot tell the difference.

1. *A spiritual vision.* A person has a vision in his spirit, or sees in his spirit. This is the first and lowest type of vision.

   Example: Saul on the road to Damascus (Acts 9:1-8). The Bible says about Saul that *". . . when his eyes were OPENED, he saw no man. . . ."* Saul's eyes were shut when he had this vision and saw Jesus. Paul didn't see the Lord with his physical eyes. He saw into the spirit realm with his eyes closed.

   Actually, the Bible says Saul was blinded for a time, so he couldn't have seen Jesus with his physical eyes. Later Ananias prayed for Paul that he might receive his sight (Acts 9:17).

2. *A trance.* Jesus pointed out to me that the second highest type of vision is when one falls into a trance.

   When one falls into a trance, his physical senses are suspended for the moment. He is not aware of where he is or anything that contacts the physical realm. He is not unconscious; he is just more conscious of spiritual things than he is of physical things.

   Examples: Paul. When Paul went to Jerusalem the first time, he said, *"And it came to pass, that, when I was come again to Jerusalem, even while I prayed in the temple, I was in a trance; And saw him [Jesus] saying unto me, Make haste, and get thee quickly out of Jerusalem: for they will not receive thy testimony concerning me"* (Acts 22:17,18).

   Peter. The tenth chapter of Acts relates the story of Peter's vision in which the Lord told him to take the

Gospel to the Gentiles. Peter went up on the housetop to pray and there ". . . *fell into a trance"* (v. 10).

When Peter fell into a trance, he ". . . *saw heaven opened . . ."* (v. 11). He was seeing into the spirit realm. We see from the Bible that both Peter and Paul fell into a trance and saw into the spirit realm.

3. *An open vision.* This is the highest type of vision. When this happens, one's physical senses are not suspended. His physical eyes are not closed. He possesses all his physical capabilities, yet he sees and hears in the realm of the spirit.

John. In chapter one of the Book of Revelation, it appears that John saw the Lord in an open vision.

Personal experience: This is the kind of vision I had when Jesus appeared to me in 1959 and taught me about the ministry of a prophet. I saw Jesus walk into my room. I heard His footsteps. I saw Him enter my room just as plainly as any man I have ever seen in my life. I saw Him sit down beside my bed. I heard His voice as plainly as any man's voice I have ever heard in my life.

e. The prophets of the Old Testament were called *seers.* They would see and know things supernaturally.

1. The Lord reminded me in that vision of the time when Saul, as a young boy, was out looking for some of his father's donkeys that had strayed away (1 Sam. 9). When Saul inquired about them, someone suggested that he go to the prophet and ask him where to find the donkeys, for the prophet Samuel would know where they were. Saul went to Samuel and was told that the donkeys had been found three days before, and that now people were out looking for Saul. Samuel knew this supernaturally.

Samuel also asked Saul to wait, for he had a word of wisdom to him concerning God's plan. Saul was then anointed to be the first king of Israel. Certainly Samuel didn't know the whereabouts of every stray donkey in Israel. There could have been many stray donkeys at that time. God had a purpose in revealing this to him at that particular time, for it concerned Israel's future king.

Personal experience: Once I stopped to visit with a minister at the site where he was building a new church. After he showed me around, we got into our cars to leave. Just as we did, the word of the Lord came unto me saying that I should tell this minister that he wasn't going to live much longer unless he judged himself in three areas: his diet, his money matters, and his lack of love for the brethren.

I stepped out of my car to go and tell him this, but someone else walked up to his car about that time and began to talk with him. I sat back down in my car and began to reason with myself. I knew that he probably would not receive this from me. He certainly didn't walk in love toward the brethren, so he would probably slap my face. As I sat there talking myself out of it, the minister left without my telling him what the Lord had shown me. That was the last time I saw him, for three years later, although a young man, he died.

f.   The word "revealed" is used in connection with the prophet's ministry.

1 CORINTHIANS 14:29,30
29 Let the prophets speak two or three, and LET THE OTHER JUDGE.
30 If any thing BE REVEALED to another that sitteth by, let the first hold his peace.

1. A prophet may speak forth his revelations through the gift of prophecy. This is on a higher level than simple prophecy.

2. A prophet may also bring forth his revelation just by telling what the Holy Spirit is saying.

3. Revelations are to be judged.

   Comments: It is scriptural for others to judge prophecy (1 Cor. 14:29). People who don't want their revelations — or prophecies — judged are wrong. And they could be into spiritual pride.

   Someone might say, "Well, the Lord doesn't make mistakes."

   Certainly not. But these spiritual gifts are being manifested through human beings who are imperfect.

   It's similar to water flowing through a pipe. Water can take on the same taste as the pipe it flows through.

   Other people have the Spirit of God, especially those who are used in this area, so that's why the Word says, "*. . . let the other judge.*"

g. Sometimes the prophet does operate in the place of *a foreteller.* This is the gift of the word of wisdom in operation through the prophet.

   1. *Agabus.*

      He foretold a drought (Acts 11:28).
      He foretold what would happen to Paul in Jerusalem (Acts 21:10,11).

h. Some do not believe that *personal prophecy* is scriptural. They do not believe that a prophet may have a message for an individual.

1. Agabus did (Acts 21:10,11). He did not tell Paul *not* to go to Jerusalem. He merely told Paul what would happen to him there, and it came to pass.

2. Many times God has shown me things along this line that have blessed and helped individuals. We need this kind of manifestation today.

3. God does show us things as He wills to prepare us and to get us ready for the future. But you cannot turn the ministry of the prophet on and off as you please. It only operates as the Spirit wills.

4. God does use people sometimes to personally minister a message to someone else. Then sometimes they think they can give everyone a message. No! *Those people who are always going around handing out personal messages and prophecies to everybody are in error and fanaticism and in dire trouble.*

Satan can mislead them. And he will do it.

i. There is a similarity between the prophet's ministry of the Old Testament and the New Testament. However, the prophet under the New Testament does not have the same status as the prophet under the Old Testament.

1. People of the Old Covenant went to the prophet for guidance. Only the king, the priest, and the prophet were anointed by the Spirit of God to stand in their respective offices.

The rest of the people had no tangible Presence of God in their lives. The Presence of God was shut up in the Holy of Holies. They didn't have the Spirit of God either on them or in them.

Unless God just saw fit to move and demonstrate Himself in the natural realm, as in the case of Gideon, people would go to the prophet for guidance.

C. *Under the New Covenant it is unscriptural to seek guidance through the ministry of the prophet.*

1. Jesus said this to me when He appeared to me in 1959.

2. We have a better covenant (Heb. 8:6).

3. We have the same Presence of God within us that was kept shut up in the Holy of Holies. He is living within us. Our bodies become the temple of God under the New Covenant (1 Cor. 3:16; 6:19; 2 Cor. 6:16).

4. He is within us to lead us.
   "For as many as are led by the Spirit of God, they are the sons of God" (Rom. 8:14).

5. Every believer needs to learn to follow the Spirit of God for himself. He shouldn't have to go to anyone else for guidance.

6. There are people who endeavor to control people's lives through personal prophecy. I don't know why they like to do it because it is unscriptural.

   Through the years I've seen this come in cycles. A lot of things happen in this day and people think they have a "new revelation." But I saw the same thing years ago. It died out then, and it will die out now because it is not founded on the Word.

   They think they have something new and really it's the spirit of deception. It is not the Holy Spirit at all.

   Through the years, I've seen so-called prophets tell people whom to marry and not to marry. I never saw one case work out right. And, oh, the tragedy I've seen in this area.

7. Know in your own spirit that God is leading you. If whatever someone else says confirms what you have in your spirit, fine. If it doesn't, forget it.

8. The prophet Agabus took Paul's girdle and bound his own hands and feet with it and said:

> **ACTS 21:11-14**
> **11 ... Thus saith the Holy Ghost, So shall the Jews at Jerusalem bind the man that owneth this girdle, and shall deliver him into the hands of the Gentiles.**
> **12 And when we heard these things, both we, and they of that place, besought him not to go up to Jerusalem.**
> **13 Then Paul answered, What mean ye to weep and to break mine heart? for I am ready not to be bound only, but also to die at Jerusalem for the name of the Lord Jesus.**
> **14 And when he would not be persuaded, we ceased, saying, The will of the Lord be done.**

Notice something. Agabus foretold what would happen. But he did not say one thing about what God's will was in the matter. Agabus didn't tell Paul to go or not to go to Jerusalem. He did not give Paul any personal direction about it. Agabus just told Paul what was out in front of him. Paul had to make his own decision whether or not God was leading him to go to Jerusalem.

Some people think Paul missed God — that the Spirit of God was telling him not to go to Jerusalem.

That cannot be the case. For when Paul was arrested while on his mission, Jesus appeared to him in the night.

> **ACTS 23:11**
> **11 And the night following the Lord stood by him, and said, Be of good cheer, Paul: for as thou hast testified of me in Jerusalem, so must thou bear witness also at Rome.**

If Paul had been out of the will of God, the Lord would have told him so.

D. *Put the Word first.* Even though there are supernatural manifestations in your life, don't build your ministry on supernatural manifestations. Invite them and have them. But *build your ministry on the Word.* Even if you're a prophet, build your ministry on the Word.

1. During the divine healing revival from 1947 through about 1958, God sent me to talk to some of the ministers. He told me to tell them, "You can't build a ministry on spiritual gifts. Develop your preaching ministry. Go ahead and operate in the spiritual gifts, but develop your preaching ministry. If you don't, you're going to wind up on the spiritual junk heap." They eventually wound up just where He said they would.

    It was Thanksgiving time 1954, and I said to them, "When you fellows have come and gone, I'll still be out there." They looked at me, startled. But now they have practically all come and gone.

    God inspired me to say this to them, trying to get them to swing back over on the Word more than just on gifts of the Spirit. I said, "You see, I'm building on the Word, not on spiritual gifts, and the Word lasts forever. It never fails."

E. *It is dangerous to feel obligated to perform.*

1. Some people who have been called of God, anointed and equipped by Him to stand in a certain office, have thought, *I'm obligated to perform.*

    So when the Holy Spirit is not in manifestation, they try to operate something themselves. THAT IS A DANGEROUS PLACE TO GET INTO.

    If the manifestation is there, fine.
    If it is not — don't try to produce it yourself.

2. God sent me to speak to one particular minister on two occasions. The Lord told me to tell him, "If the manifestation is there, fine. If it is not, go ahead and preach and forget it."

The Lord told me to tell him, "If you don't, you're going to wind up on the spiritual junk heap." I'm sorry to say he did. He wouldn't listen. He told me, "I feel like I'm obligated to perform." I said, "Well, if you're performing, you missed it to begin with."

I was 36 at the time. I went from there to Scranton, Pennsylvania, and then to New Jersey for a two-week meeting with Brother A. A. Swift, a great man of God, then 72.

I told Brother Swift what the Lord told me to tell the other minister. Brother Swift said, "The word of knowledge operates through him. I recognize it. But I spent a long time in China and became acquainted with occult powers." He said, "What some of the brethren don't realize is that if the Spirit of God is not in manifestation and you move out in that area and try to do something in the flesh, you are throwing yourself wide open for deception by occult powers. This is because, you see, you have left the Word."

F. *Discern the difference* between the Spirit of God and familiar spirits.

  1. There is no use being scared off because of evil spirits — actually it is familiar spirits which are operating. They are familiar with people and they communicate with the one through whom they operate.

  2. When God led Israel out of Egypt, you remember that Aaron threw down his rod and it turned into a serpent. The magicians did the same thing — they threw down their rods and they turned into serpents. However, Aaron's rod swallowed up the magicians' rods (Exod. 7:12).

  3. The devil knows some things. But he is not all-knowing like God. But the Bible talks about familiar spirits. They are here. And they are familiar with you — even though you are saved and filled with the Holy Spirit. If someone is in contact with them, they will tell him things about you.

The little maiden Paul cast the devil out of had a spirit of divination — a spirit of divining (Acts 16:16-19). That means foretelling or fortune telling, but it is the wrong kind of spirit.

The devil knows things that are going to happen to people if they keep walking just like they are. If they're his children, he knows exactly what's going to happen to them.

4. I know a certain person through whom the word of knowledge supposedly operated. He'd know things about people. He would just rattle off the revelation he had received about people.

When he came to one of my meetings once, the pastor asked him to greet the congregation. While he was speaking, I heard the Holy Spirit speak up and say, "Familiar spirits." I knew the Lord was telling me that familiar spirits were operating through him.

In the process of time, in another part of the country, a good friend of mine asked me, "Do you know So-and-so?" calling this "minister's" name. "Yes," I said, "I know who he is, but I'm not acquainted with him." "Well," he said, "I thought he was a real man of God because of that supernatural something which operates through him. And I was taken in by him. I had a very valuable piece of jewelry I had inherited which I kept in a certain place in my home. That fellow stood in my office, described the diamond exactly, told me where I kept it, and said that the Lord wanted me to give it to him.

"I thought it was God," he said, "because it was supernatural. So I got it and gave it to him.

"But it wasn't two days later that he stood right here in my same office, lost his temper, and cursed out a man. Then before he got out of town — this isn't hearsay — I know it for a fact — he got tangled up with another fellow in homosexuality and misled some boys and got them into difficulty."

Then I shared with him what God had already shown me. I said, "He has familiar spirits. It's not the Spirit of God operating through him."

5. *How can you tell the difference?*

    a. From First Corinthians 12:1-3.

        1 CORINTHIANS 12:1-3
        1 Now concerning spiritual gifts, brethren, I would not have you ignorant.
        2 Ye know that ye were Gentiles, carried away unto these dumb idols, EVEN AS YE WERE LED.
        3 Wherefore I give you to understand, that no man speaking by the Spirit of God calleth Jesus accursed: and that NO MAN CAN SAY THAT JESUS IS THE LORD, BUT BY THE HOLY GHOST.

        Interpret this scripture in context. Paul is writing about spiritual manifestations and things pertaining to the Holy Spirit. Of course, a person could say, "Jesus is Lord" out of his head. A rank sinner could say that. But what this scripture is saying is, *when the Holy Spirit is in manifestation, He always makes Jesus Lord.* When it is the Holy Spirit in manifestation, He says Jesus is Lord. *The Holy Spirit doesn't attract attention unto man and make man Lord.*

    b. Does the manifestation bring glory to Jesus? Does it bring blessing to people? Does it bring them nearer to God?

    c. Or does it exalt man? Does it attract attention to the human?

6. There's no use being scared off because of evil spirits. GOD CAN TOP ANYTHING THE DEVIL CAN DO. The manifestations of the Holy Spirit are real. Let's have the real manifestations that will bless people.

7. Be open to God and invite the Spirit of God to manifest Himself among us in the various and the varied ministries that He set in the Church.

59

G. *Misconceptions* people have relative to the prophet's office.

1. *Many think that a prophet is supposed to do nothing but prophesy.*
    But the foremost ministry of the prophet is to preach or teach the
    Word.

    a. *A prophet does more than prophesy.* In fact, very often when
        he is giving forth the revelation of the moment he is not
        prophesying at all — he is just telling what was revealed to
        him. For example, Agabus "signified by the Spirit" that there
        would be a great drought (Acts 11:28).

    b. *A prophet does more than have revelations.*
        People get into error who think, *I'm called to be a prophet*
        (and they might be) so they're always trying to have a reve-
        lation, or always trying to prophesy.

    c. *Before anything else, a prophet would be a preacher or a
        teacher of the Word.* Jesus said John the Baptist was a great
        prophet, yet we have no record that John ever *foretold* any-
        thing. Rather, he *forthtold* or *preached* the message of the
        Kingdom of God under the inspiration of the Holy Spirit.

    d. *The laying on of hands goes with the prophet's ministry.*

    e. *A healing ministry goes along with the prophet's office.*

    And when the prophet exercises the gifts of healings (or any
    ministry function), it is a prophet's ministry in operation.

    1. *Elisha.* Jesus said:

        LUKE 4:27
        **27 And many lepers were in Israel in the
        time of Eliseus the prophet; and none of
        them was cleansed, saving Naaman the
        Syrian.**
        Elisha had a healing ministry. And people knew about

it. The reason Naaman came to Elisha was that a little Jewish maiden was captured by Syria in a war against Israel. She was a slave in Naaman's home. When she learned Naaman had leprosy, she said, ". . . *Would God my lord were with the prophet that is in Samaria! for he would recover him of his leprosy*" (2 Kings 5:3).

2. *Jesus.* Jesus stood in the office of prophet. His healing ministry exemplifies all the varied manifestations you would not see in just one person's ministry.

3. A prophet's healing ministry can operate through the laying on of hands.

4. It can also operate in various other ways.
   a. Elisha didn't lay hands on Naaman. He didn't even go out to see him. *He had a word from the Lord.* He sent a messenger saying, ". . . *Go and wash in Jordan seven times, and thy flesh shall come again to thee, and thou shalt be clean*" (2 Kings 5:10).

   b. Jesus ministered healing through laying on of hands.

   But He also ministered healing by other methods. For example, without touching ten lepers, Jesus said to them, "Go and show yourselves to the high priests." As they went, they were healed (Luke 17:12-14).

   Jesus spit on the ground and made clay of the spittle and rubbed it on a blind man's eyes and said, "Go wash it off in the pool of Siloam" (John 9:6,7). Why did He do that? Because the Spirit of God told Him to. He was standing in the office of the prophet. Gifts of healings were operating through Him.

Jesus was anointed with the healing power of God (Acts 10:38). And on other occasions, Jesus ministered healing by the transfer of power. In other words, people were also healed when the healing anointing flowed out of Jesus into them. The woman with the issue of blood is an example (Mark 5:25-34). (*See* also Matthew 14:34-36; Mark 6:56; Luke 6:19.)

5. Concerning the healing of Naaman through the ministry of the prophet Elisha, Jesus said, *"And many lepers were in Israel in the time of Eliseus the prophet; and none of them was cleansed, saving Naaman the Syrian"* (Luke 4:27).

    Why couldn't Elisha get all the lepers in Israel healed? Naaman was a heathen; he wasn't even an Israelite. He wasn't in covenant with God. He worshiped the idol Dagon.

    Why couldn't Elisha tell all the lepers of Israel, including those who were in covenant with God, "Go dip in the River Jordan seven times and your flesh will come again clean as a little child"?

    Because God didn't tell him to!

    You cannot go beyond the word of the Lord.
    The word of the Lord, no doubt, came unto Elisha and told him what to do in the case of Naaman.

    Personal experience: People are healed that way today. I've had many healed that way — by the Word of the Lord in a supernatural manifestation of the Holy Spirit. Yet I couldn't make it work for others. The Lord told me exactly what to do. Sometimes He told me what to tell people to do. Sometimes I would see it in vision form, then go out and act it out in the church meeting. And people have gotten up and walked off stretchers.

Yet others in the same meeting were rolled in on stretchers, and rolled out on them.

Some people who are not knowledgeable about the Bible said, "That couldn't be God. If He healed one, He would have healed the others too."

In the first place, I wasn't doing the healing. In the second place, I had no word from the Lord on the others. The others could have been healed if they would have believed God and made contact with Him on their own, but somehow or another they did not.

2. *Many think that a prophet should always know everything about everyone and everything that is happening round about him.*

   a. *That could not be so.* For if it had been so, Gehazi, the servant of Elisha, would have known he didn't stand one chance in a million of getting by with what he did (2 Kings 5:20-27).

Naaman offered the prophet Elisha gifts after his healing was manifested. Elisha would not accept them. So Naaman went happily on his way back to Syria. But Gehazi ran after him and lied to him. He said, "My master has sent me. After you left two young prophets came. And although my master wouldn't take anything for himself, he said it would be all right to take a talent of silver and two changes of garments for them" (2 Kings 5:22).

Naaman, thrilled about being healed from such a terrible condition, gave Gehazi more than he asked for. Gehazi took it and hid it.

But when Gehazi got into the presence of his master, Elisha asked him where he had been. Gehazi answered, ". . . *Thy servant went no wither*" (2 Kings 5:25). And Elisha said unto him, ". . . *Went not mine heart with thee, when the man turned again from his chariot. . . ?*"

However, if Elisha had always known everything about everyone and all that was going on around him, Gehazi, who was with Elisha continually, would have known that. And Gehazi would never have tried what he did.

    b.   *The Lord only tells a prophet what He wants him to know. He does not tell a prophet everything.*

Other Scriptures also indicate that the prophet does not know everything. For example, when the Shunammite woman came to Elisha the prophet and caught him by the feet after her son had died, Elisha said, "... *her soul is vexed within her: and THE LORD HATH HID IT FROM ME, and hath not told me*" (2 Kings 4:27).

3.   *Some think that because one is a prophet, they can ask him at any time, "Have you got a word for me?"*

    a.   You cannot conjure up these things as you will.

    b.   God may give you a word and He may not. The majority of times He will not.

Personal comments: The word of knowledge, the word of wisdom, discerning of spirits, as well as prophecy, operate in the office of the prophet. Because these are spiritual gifts, they will also operate in the life of any Spirit-filled believer as the need may arise or as the Lord wills. But the occasional operation of these gifts does not make one a prophet.

Almost immediately after I was filled with the Spirit and began to speak with other tongues, the word of knowledge began to operate in my life. I would see and know things supernaturally. But that didn't make me a prophet.

I was 20 years old and the pastor of a country community church, when two weeks after I was baptized in the Holy Spirit, I had a quick spiritual vision — I call it a "mini-vision." I saw a person in the congregation and I saw how she had been pushed into sin two nights before. Although she was forced into it, this young woman was thinking, *I've sinned and God doesn't love me anymore.* Her friend had insisted she come to church that night, but she had already decided never to come back again. As I started to dismiss the service and shut my eyes to pray, I saw all of this: who she was with, what she had done, and how it had happened. I made it known to her in a way the congregation wouldn't know she was the one I was talking about. I used wisdom in order to avoid embarrassing her.

(If you do have a revelation, seek God for wisdom on how to handle it properly. Don't just blurt it out. It is possible to shipwreck people's lives and mess things up so that God won't give you further revelation.

You can grieve the Spirit of God so He won't show you anything else because He can't trust you.)

The young woman, convinced of God's love and forgiveness for her, rushed to the altar in tears. *God had revealed this to me to save her.*

Sometime later, but before I was married, I was pastoring a Full Gospel church. There was a beautiful young lady in the church who was quite interested in me, and I was a little bit interested in her.

We had Saturday night, Sunday morning, and Sunday night services. Because she was the most talented singer we had, she usually sang a special. But one particular Saturday night she was not there to sing.

The next morning I was already in the pulpit preaching the Sunday service when I looked out the window and saw a car drive up. I saw her get out of the car and come down the side aisle of the church. The man who was driving the car drove quickly away.

Suddenly, I was no longer in the service. I heard the sound of my voice as it went right on speaking, but I didn't know what I was saying. My spirit was somewhere else. I know what Elisha meant when he said, "My spirit went with you."

All of a sudden, I was standing on the street in a town 15 miles from where I was preaching that Sunday morning. It was Saturday night. This was the '30s. The streets were thick with people. In those days, all the country people came to town on Saturday night.

I stood in front of a store right on the main street. I saw this young woman come walking down the street. I saw the same car pull up to the curb beside her. When the driver sounded the horn, she got into the car with him.

Then instead of standing in front of the store, in the Spirit, I was sitting in the back seat of the car. He drove out into the country, and they committed adultery.

God showed me that to protect me. Several times He showed me things to help others. But those revelations didn't make me a prophet.

I had been preaching nearly 20 years when Jesus appeared to me in a vision in 1952, and said, "From this time forward, what is known in My Word as discerning of spirits will operate in your life and ministry when you are in the spirit."

When discerning of spirits began to operate in my life, I could see and hear in the realm of the spirit. Then two revelation gifts — discerning of spirits and the word of knowledge — operated in my life on a consistent basis, plus prophecy. That's when I stepped into the prophetic office. But, even then, I didn't stand in the prophet's office publicly until 1953.
If God did call you to an office, you couldn't step into it immediately. You'd make a mess of it if you did. But God will add a little here and a little there. If He does have in mind to put you in that office, eventually, if you'll be faithful, when He sees He can trust you with it, He will set you in it.

God will not violate the principles set forth in His own Word. The Spirit of God said through Paul not to put a novice in office, "*. . . lest being lifted up with pride he fall into the condemnation of the devil*" (1 Tim. 3:6).

The same is true in other offices. If novices were put into these offices, Satan would tempt them and they would be lifted up and destroyed. I think some have been destroyed because they sensed in their spirits the calling, but instead of waiting for God to set them into that office, they tried to set themselves into it.

I can see the wisdom of God in my own ministry. As a younger person and immature mentally as well as spiritually, if I had been thrust into some offices and places I fill now, I would never have made it. I would have fallen by the wayside. When God used me, my head would have gotten so big I couldn't have walked out of the door.

I'm glad God can use us. But I don't get lifted up in any way when He does. It humbles me for God to use me. I don't get the least bit of pride. I don't even get excited or show emotion over a lot of things. I just say, "What of it? After all, I read in the Old Testament that God spoke Hebrew through a donkey. That didn't make the donkey anything special. So if God sees fit to use this donkey, praise the Lord, *God* did it. Give Him all the glory."

Don't be taken up with names and titles.

And don't go out and say, "I'm a prophet." You may be one day, and then again you may not be. But if you are called to the prophetic office, let God set you into it. Don't try to set yourself in a particular office.

Don't even necessarily say, "I'm a teacher." God may want to make an evangelist out of you. Wait and find out what God wants you to do.

The Evangelist

EPHESIANS 4:11,12
11 And he gave some, apostles; and some, prophets; AND SOME, EVANGELISTS; and some, pastors and teachers; 12 For the perfecting of the saints, for the work of the ministry, for the edifying of the body of Christ.

1 CORINTHIANS 12:28
28 And God hath set some in the church, first apostles, secondarily prophets, thirdly teachers, after that MIRA-CLES, then GIFTS OF HEALINGS, helps, governments, diversities of tongues.

A. The word "evangelist" occurs only three times in the New Testament.

1. In Ephesians 4:11, quoted above.

2. In Acts 21:8 the Bible speaks of "Philip the evangelist."

3. In Second Timothy 4:5, Paul told Timothy, who was the pastor of a New Testament church at the time, to "do the work of an evangelist."

B. The meaning of the word "evangelist" is: *One who brings the evangel (the good news); a messenger of good tidings.*

C. The evangelist brings the message of the redeeming grace of God.

D. The evangelist's favorite theme is salvation in its simplest form.

E. The only New Testament example we have of an evangelist is Philip. Philip's ministry is the model because it is the only one God gave us.

1. Philip had just one message, and that was Jesus Christ.

   a. Philip's message to Samaria:

      ACTS 8:5
      5 Then Philip went down to the city of Samaria, AND PREACHED CHRIST UNTO THEM.

   b. Philip's message to the eunuch:

      ACTS 8:35
      35 Then Philip opened his mouth, and began at the same scripture, and PREACHED UNTO HIM JESUS.

   c. One notable characteristic of evangelists is this: No matter what scripture they begin with, they preach Jesus. That is their calling. That is their message.

F. The supernatural equipment accompanying the evangelist's ministry includes "miracles" and "gifts of healings."

1. The evangelist is plainly a direct endowment or ministry gift from the Lord (Eph. 4:11). Yet in First Corinthians 12:28, the evangelist is not mentioned by name in this list. (Neither is the pastor mentioned by name in this list. The apostle is. The prophet is. The teacher is. But the evangelist and the pastor are not.)

2. I believe the evangelist is mentioned in the First Corinthians 12:28 list when it says "miracles, then gifts of healings."

a. Miracles and gifts of healings can also go with other offices, but we know from the only New Testament model, Philip, that they should accompany the evangelist's ministry.

> **ACTS 8:5-8**
> **5 Then Philip went down to the city of Samaria, and preached Christ unto them.**
> **6 And the people with one accord gave heed unto those things which Philip spake, HEARING AND SEEING THE MIRACLES WHICH HE DID.**
> **7 For unclean spirits, crying with loud voice, came out of many that were possessed with them: and many taken with palsies, and that were lame, WERE HEALED.**
> **8 And there was great joy in that city.**

b. Healings followed the preaching of Christ. If, as the Scripture says, *"Himself took our infirmities, and bare our sicknesses,"* you could not preach Christ in His fullness without preaching the healing part of our redemption also.

3. In my opinion, what we call an "evangelist" many times is an "exhorter."

a. There is the ministry of exhortation (Rom. 12:8).

b. An "exhorter" exhorts people to be saved.

c. The supernatural equipment of miracles and gifts of healings does not follow the ministry of exhortation.

d. One may start out as an exhorter and as he proves faithful, God may set him in the office of the evangelist later.

G. If the divine gift or endowment is within a person, the person will need no pleading to be an evangelist. There will be a divine urge burning within him or her.

1. Philip is first seen as a deacon (a helper) in the church (Acts 6:1-6). It would be safe to say that the apostles ordained Philip as a deacon, but they gave him no commission to evangelize. Yet we see him down in Samaria with this heavenly gift burning in his spirit, which urged him to preach the Gospel with glorious results.

2. Paul said, *". . . woe is unto me, if I preach not the gospel!"* (1 Cor. 9:16). If one really has a divine call burning within him, no matter what the office, he will say like Paul, "Woe is me if I preach not the Gospel!"

3. God told Jeremiah to prophesy against Israel. God also told Jeremiah no one would listen and that he wouldn't have any followers. Jeremiah grew weary and once said, in effect, "I'm not going to prophesy anymore unto this people. I'm not going to speak anymore in His Name." (We would say, "I'm not going to preach anymore.") Then Jeremiah said, *". . . But his word was in mine heart as a burning fire shut up in my bones . . ."* (Jer. 20:9).

H. *The marks of a true evangelist* are evident in the ministry of Philip, our one New Testament model:

1. *Supernatural advertisement.*

   a. There was something to see and hear in Philip's ministry: *"And the people with one accord gave heed unto those things which Philip spake, HEARING and SEEING the MIRACLES which he did"* (Acts 8:6).

   b. Philip the evangelist was equipped with the particular spiritual gifts needed for his ministry — working of miracles and gifts of healings. The display of these spiritual gifts through him is the finest form of advertising there can be.

2. *True evangelists must preach the Word.*

   a. In the ministry of the evangelist, the preaching of the Word of God is essential.

b. Divine power will draw a crowd. Miracles and healings arrest and compel people's attention. But it is in believing the Word that men are saved.

> **ACTS 8:12**
> **12 But WHEN THEY BELIEVED PHILIP PREACHING the things concerning the kingdom of God, and the name of Jesus Christ, they were baptized, both men and women.**

    1. Miracles and healings were mentioned earlier (vv. 6,7). The people saw these things in demonstration. But the Bible does *not* say people were saved, "When they believed what they SAW. . . ." It says they were saved, "When they believed Philip PREACHING. . . ."

    2. No one was saved until Philip preached the Word. People were saved as a result of his preaching.

c. Paul told Timothy (and remember Paul also told Timothy to do the work of an evangelist), "Preach the Word" (2 Tim. 4:2).

d. Only the preaching of the Word affects the will of the sinner.

3. *Individual decision.*

a. Conversion is an individual matter. It is something personal between the human spirit and God.

b. God is trying to get something over to us when He records the mass conversions in Samaria, and then He finishes the chapter with the account of the evangelist and the Ethiopian — one person.

c. The supreme gift of a real evangelist is the power to bring a person's soul to a decision for Christ.

4. *The evangelist's need for others.*

    a. The diversity of ministry gifts God has set in the Church are dependent upon one another for their fullest expression and most lasting results.

    b. Sending Peter and John to Samaria is significant in this regard.

> **ACTS 8:14**
> **14 Now when the apostles which were at Jerusalem heard that Samaria had received the word of God, they sent unto them Peter and John.**

    1. As an evangelist, Philip had the ability to get people saved, but his ministry did not extend beyond bringing people into salvation.

    2. Philip had no ability to establish a church, or to get people rooted and grounded in the Word, or to teach them.

    3. He seemingly did not have the ministry to impart the baptism in the Holy Spirit that Peter and John had (vv. 14-17).

    4. Philip did his job in getting the people to God by preaching salvation through Jesus Christ. Then the apostles sent others to take them on in God.

    c. One person will never be able to do everything. And he should not. All of us are limited. Every minister is limited. But God is not limited. That's why we need one another.

    d. Howard Carter was a great pioneer of the Pentecostal Movement. He founded the first Pentecostal Bible school in the world. It still exists in England. The revelation God gave him concerning the gifts and manifestations of the Holy Spirit as recorded in First Corinthians 12 is regarded as fundamental truth today.

I had read after him for years but had never met him personally, when I had an opportunity to attend one of his meetings.

Rev. Carter had a ministry of laying on of hands to get people filled with the Holy Spirit.

After the service, he told the pastor and me that on the two-year trip around the world he had just completed (God had told him to go and minister to missionaries), he had laid hands on 645 denominational missionaries and heard them speak with other tongues.

That night when I heard him preach, 19 people had come to be filled with the Spirit, and in 10 minutes' time Rev. Carter laid hands on them and all 19 began speaking in tongues.

Afterward as we stood talking together in the back of the church, a woman came up and asked, "Brother Carter, would you pray for my healing?"

He smiled and said, "No, sister. I would if no one else were here. But that's not my ministry. God primarily uses me to lay hands on people to be filled with the Holy Spirit. But He uses my wife in healing. Seldom do people fail to receive healing, when she lays hands on them. So she lays hands on people for healing, and I lay hands on them to receive the Holy Spirit. You go to my wife and have her pray for your healing."

He recognized that he was limited.

He could have laid hands on her in faith as any believer can do. But there are people who are specially endowed by the Spirit of God with a healing anointing to minister to others.

Some might be endowed to both lay hands on people to receive the Holy Spirit and to receive healing, but Carter was not. He recognized his limitations and he recognized another's ministry.

Not one of us is all-sufficient. We need one another.

I.   The evangelist's ministry is more of a roving ministry, ministering to the unsaved.

The Pastor

EPHESIANS 4:11

11 And he gave some, apostles; and some, prophets; and some, evangelists; and some, PASTORS. . . .

A.   The word "pastor" is used only once in the *King James* translation of the New Testament. And that is here in Ephesians 4:11.

This seems strange when we realize that the office of pastor is probably the most widely recognized office in Christian ministry today.

Yet I am certain there are many references to this "pastoral" office.

B.   The Greek word translated "pastor" literally means "shepherd."

C.   It is so translated referring to our Lord and Savior, the Lord Jesus Christ, who is the Great Example of a true pastor or shepherd:

JOHN 10:11

11 I am the GOOD SHEPHERD: the GOOD SHEPHERD giveth his life for the sheep.

HEBREWS 13:20
20 Now the God of peace, that brought again from the dead our Lord Jesus, THAT GREAT SHEPHERD of the sheep. . . .

1 PETER 2:25
25 For ye were as sheep going astray; but are now returned unto the SHEPHERD AND BISHOP of your souls.

1 PETER 5:4
4 And when the CHIEF SHEPHERD shall appear, ye shall receive a crown of glory that fadeth not away.

D. *Jesus is the Great Shepherd, the Chief Shepherd, of all God's sheep.*

E. Jesus has undershepherds. *A pastor is an undershepherd.* A pastor is a shepherd of God's sheep in the local body.

F. God calls men and equips them to shepherd, or pastor, a flock.

G. Shepherds are necessary for the maturing and equipping of the saints.

　　1.　In New Testament days, as believers began to gather together in recognized local churches, groups, or assemblies, they needed certain ones to exercise a position of loving oversight and care. That's the position of the pastor or the shepherd.

　　2.　Jesus had compassion upon people "scattered abroad, as sheep having no shepherd" (Matt. 9:36).

　　　　a.　Sheep without shepherds are scattered abroad — *they go astray.*

　　　　b.　We see this in groups where there is no shepherd.

H. This office is a more settled or stationary office.

　　1.　A person called to be a shepherd or pastor to a flock would be more or less settled in the locality of the flock he is to oversee.

I. *The shepherd (pastor) has oversight of the flock.*

1. Jesus is the Great Shepherd. He is the *Head*, the *Overseer*, of the whole Church — the Body of Christ. The pastor is the undershepherd. He is the *head* or the *overseer* of the local flock or group. The local body heads up in the pastor. The head *governs*. *Therefore, the governing ability of the local body heads up in the pastoral or shepherd's office.*

2. The office of pastor is not mentioned by name in First Corinthians 12:28. But "governments" is listed. I believe in this list of ministry gifts that God has set in the Church, "governments" is the pastor's office.

3. Is it scriptural for deacon boards or boards of elders to run the local church?

    a. In the early days of the Church when the Church was in the babyhood stage of development, the assemblies were put in the charge of local elders until ministry gifts could develop.

        The Greek word translated "elder" simply means an older person. These elders were older people, fitted to a place of position and responsibility.

        The only ministries the Church had at first were the twelve Apostles of the Lamb. A novice could not be set in as a pastor or shepherd of the flock (1 Tim. 3:6). So until some of those newly saved converts were called into the ministry by God and had developed into pastors — and this takes time — older men with more maturity, both mentally and in character, were put in charge of the flock.

        We don't have this situation today. The Church is no longer in an infancy stage of development. Ministry gifts have already been developed in the Church.

It has created problems when people have said, "We want a New Testament church. Let's go back to the Acts of the Apostles." Then they appointed elders to run the church.

(Yes, we are to get back to the Acts of the Apostles in doctrine and in the demonstration of the Holy Spirit. In other words, the same Holy Ghost experiences that were available to those in the Early Church are available to us too. But if we do as the Early Church did *in practice* in their formative stage of government, we will stay in a babyhood state of Christianity. The New Testament clearly reveals God's plan for the Church — that it grow up!)

Such elders appointed by men today have no call of God upon them. They know nothing about the pastoral office, because the *call* is not there; the *anointing* is not there.

It is unscriptural to appoint elders to oversee a flock and to run a church when there is a pastor to oversee it.

That is reverting back to the babyhood stage of development as in the Early Church and acknowledging, "We've never grown beyond that. We're all spiritual babies."

Personal comments: I have been in the ministry for more than half a century and I have observed this. I have never seen a church yet that really had the power of God in operation and did what God called them to do unless the pastor really had the oversight and say-so of the local body. When a deacon board, or a board of elders, or any other kind of board had the say-so and ran the church, I've never seen one yet that functioned correctly, or where the power of God hadn't waned.

You can go into those churches and try to preach, but something is not right. I illustrate it like this — it's like trying to wash your feet with your socks on. God blesses them as far as He can because He loves them. But He cannot bless them in His fullest measure, because He cannot put His approval on man's ideas.

4. *Overseer.* Originally in the Early Church, the term "elders" had special reference to age, maturity, and standing. Then as ministry gifts developed in the Early Church, the more official title of "overseer" or "bishop" was used, which referred to those who were called and anointed by God to stand in the pastoral office.

    Both "overseer" and "bishop" are translated from the same Greek word, *episkopos.* It conveys a meaning of definite leadership and official position.

    a. The Greek word *episkopos* is translated "overseer" in Paul's admonition to the elders of the Church at Ephesus:

        ACTS 20:28
        28 Take heed therefore unto yourselves, and to all the flock, over the which the Holy Ghost hath made you OVERSEERS, TO FEED THE CHURCH OF GOD, which he hath purchased with his own blood.

        In order to have fed the Church of God with the Word, these people must have been teachers who were spiritually equipped to feed the flock. They could not have been just older persons who oversaw what was happening, but had no anointing or call to the ministry. But then, over the course of time, some of these elders or older men who were put over the flocks did develop into ministry gifts because they had the call of God on them. God made ministers out of them.

    b. The Greek word *episkopos* is translated "bishop" here:

        1 TIMOTHY 3:1
        1 This is a true saying, If a man desire the OFFICE OF A BISHOP, he desireth a good work.

Remember, *episkopos* is translated "overseer" elsewhere. This is talking about the pastoral ministry. The pastor or shepherd would naturally have the oversight of the flock.

1. The picture used in the Bible for the pastoral office is that of a shepherd and a flock. The shepherd is the leader of the flock. The shepherd doesn't get up in the morning and say, "We'd better get some of the chief sheep together and get their opinion as to where we'll graze today." No, the shepherd has the oversight of the sheep. He is the overseer of the flock. He heads out, and the flock follows him.

2. Notice First Timothy 3:1 calls it the "office of a bishop" (or overseer), which is referring to the pastoral office. If this office is not the pastoral office, then it is an office Jesus didn't set in the Church because all the ministry gifts are listed in Ephesians 4:11. There aren't any others. No, this office of *bishop* must of necessity be the *pastoral* office because that is the ministry gift that has the oversight of the flock.

> **1 TIMOTHY 3:2,3**
> **2 A bishop then must be blameless, the husband of one wife, vigilant, sober, of good behaviour, given to hospitality, APT TO TEACH;**
> **3 Not given to wine, no striker, NOT GREEDY OF FILTHY LUCRE. . . .**

3. It is the duty of the flock to support the pastor. But the pastor is not to serve for filthy lucre. His motive must be to serve God and to put the people first.

> **1 TIMOTHY 3:3-5**
> **3 . . . but patient, not a brawler, not covetous;**

> 4 One that ruleth well his own house,
> having his children in subjection with all
> gravity;
> 5 (For if a man know not how to rule his
> own house, how shall he take care of THE
> CHURCH OF GOD?)

4. This is definitely the office of the pastor.

> 1 TIMOTHY 3:6
> 6 NOT A NOVICE, lest being lifted up
> with pride he fall into the condemnation
> of the devil.

5. *Not a novice.* You can see they could not have had the pastoral office to begin with because initially the Early Church was in its infancy and the believers *were* novices, except for the Apostles of the Lamb. It took time for God to develop these ministries, including the pastoral ministry.

c. We see the overseer's office here again, which heads up in the pastor's office:

> 1 TIMOTHY 5:17
> 17 Let the ELDERS that rule well be
> counted worthy of double honour, espe-
> cially they who labour IN THE WORD and
> DOCTRINE.

1. The Church here is growing out of the babyhood stage of development. By this time, elders or older men who were appointed to oversee the flock had developed into ministry gifts.

2. Those who "labor in the Word and doctrine" are preachers and teachers. Some of the elders or older men had developed and matured spiritually and had the call of God on their lives so they could stand in the pastoral office and deal in the Word and in doctrine.

3. Really, the Early Church came to the place where the other elders — older men with no anointing or call to the ministry — were no longer needed in this position.

5. *It is important to see that the Early Church started out as a baby church. Babies always — whether spiritually or in the natural — outgrow babyhood characteristics. But it takes time.*

   a. In the early days of the Pentecostal Movement in this century, in some instances almost of necessity, the Church had to revert back to the babyhood stage of government as in the Acts of the Apostles.

   The older pioneers would go into areas where there were no Full Gospel churches for many miles.

   One man told me that he preached all summer in one place and got 285 people saved and about 90 of them baptized in the Holy Spirit.

   He was an evangelist — not a pastor. But he stayed with them three months, running meetings every night, and got a church started. When he left there was no pastor available, so he appointed some of the older men to oversee the flock until a pastor was developed by God and placed in the church.

   Sometimes it was two or three years before some of these new flocks had pastors.

J. *The pastor is one of the most important offices.*

   1. Without the ministry gift of pastor operating in the Body of Christ, then all other ministry is practically in vain. No matter how great the evangelist is and how many he gets saved, if there is not someone to shepherd the lambs — to pastor and take them on in God — they're apt to fall by the wayside.

It's the same way in the natural realm. No matter how many babies are born in a large city hospital, if someone doesn't care for them, they will die.

2. No other office is given so much instruction in the New Testament as is the pastoral office. Virtually no instruction is given to the apostle. No instruction is given to the evangelist. Little instruction is given to the other offices. But when you consider that *elder, overseer,* and *bishop* are all referring to the pastoral office, more direct instruction is given to the office of pastor than to any other office.

3. There is not a higher, more respected, or more needed office that God could call you to than the office of pastor. It is a noble cause.

Personal comments: You have to function where God calls you. But to be honest, if I had my desire about it, I'd rather fill this office than any other.

This is the only office I ever sought. And if I were a young person, I would seek this office. Let God do what He wants to, but I would talk to Him about it. I did. And to me He said no because of my particular call.

K. *It is the Holy Spirit who makes men overseers, not man.*

L. *God has provided supernatural equipment for the pastor.* The pastor should be equipped with supernatural equipment.

1. The gifts of the Spirit (1 Corinthians 12) can be manifested in the lives of individual members of the Body of Christ. But I'm also convinced that these supernatural gifts are the supernatural equipment for those who stand in ministry gift offices.

2. *I am convinced that the pastor ought to be equipped with the word of wisdom, the word of knowledge, and even with tongues and interpretation.*

I am also convinced that if he is not, if he will ask for that spiritual equipment, he will get it. I did.

a. Sometimes these gifts are not as spectacular in display through the pastor as they are through the prophet, although they are in operation.

b. *Pastoring supernaturally.*

1. A young man with only an eighth grade education was saved during a revival I preached. Later he was baptized in the Holy Spirit. Then he felt called to preach. While still working in a sawmill, he would go out and preach on weekends. He had no training at all except in his own church. I taught several seminars there. Soon he had so many calls to minister that he quit his job and went out full time. He spent 18 months as an evangelist. Then his home church was without a pastor, and they asked him to fill in as the pastor for three months. At the end of three months, they elected him as the pastor. And the church grew bigger than it had ever been.

I went back to preach there, and I marveled at the ability of that fellow — a man with very little education and no formal ministerial training.

They had put up a single partition in one large room to create an office for him and an adjoining sitting room. I would wait and pray in the smaller room before the services. In the daytime, I sometimes used that room to study.

Through that thin wall, I couldn't help but overhear him as he counseled people. At that time I had been in the ministry 25 years — I had pastored 12 years and had traveled in field ministry 13 years. He'd been in the ministry about four years. As people came to him with certain needs and asked him certain questions, I'd think to myself, *How in the world is he going to answer that?* I wouldn't know how!

Then the words that came out of that man's mouth would amaze me. I knew the Spirit of God was operating through him. It held me spellbound. I sat there almost wide-eyed with my mouth open as I thought, *That's a miracle of God.*

After several years he moved to a larger church. He invited me to come there. By this time he'd been in the ministry about 10 years. I almost followed him around, just listening to him. I knew he had little education and no formal training. Yet the words of wisdom, and the answers that came out of his mouth amazed me. I knew the Spirit of God had given it to him.

2. Brother O. B. Braune pastored the old Rosen Heights Assembly in Fort Worth for more than 40 years before he retired. I heard someone ask him in a question-and-answer period at a sectional meeting, "How can you pastor one church so long? What is the secret of your success?" He replied, "In my opinion, the greatest secret of pastoral work is to have the right answer for people when they come to you for help."

To do that you would have to depend upon the Spirit of God to give you the right answer.

3. I preached for Brother and Sister J. R. Goodwin in several churches they pastored. They pastored supernaturally more than any pastors I've ever known. When anyone in their church needed help, they knew it immediately by the Spirit of God.

4. I pastored that way. I never had a visitation program. I always knew on the inside in my spirit when someone in my congregation needed help.

One of the most outstanding incidents along this line happened in the last church I pastored. A building contractor had been saved just two weeks earlier. I was shaving one morning when the Spirit of God spoke to me and said, "I want you to go restore Sam. He got angry on the job yesterday and cursed. Today he's home sick in bed. He thinks God doesn't love him anymore because he failed. I want you to go restore him."

I walked out of the bathroom with half my face still lathered and said to my wife, "Honey, before I can run that errand for you, I've got to go restore Sam." And I told her what the Lord had said to me.

I finished shaving and walked into the bedroom to finish dressing. I had tied my tie and was reaching for my coat when a car drove up outside. I heard my wife let someone in, and I walked toward the living room, putting on my coat.

Sam's wife stood in our living room crying. She said, "Oh, Brother Hagin, don't tell Sam I came by here, but he's home in bed sick today." She explained that an old chronic back injury had come back on him again, and he couldn't get out of bed. Then she said, "He said he's never going back to church again. He lost his temper on the job yesterday, and some of the men said he cursed. He doesn't remember if he did or not. But he said God doesn't love him because he failed. Would you go talk to him?"

I said to her, "You can ask my wife — I'm just on my way to go talk to Sam. I've already told her I'm going. The Lord just spoke to me about him and told me what happened on the job yesterday. I'll go restore him."

When I got out to their home, I knocked on the side door where his bedroom was. He said, "Come in." When he saw me, he was so embarrassed, he pulled the sheet up over his head. And there he lay, a grown man 43 years old, holding the covers over his head, sobbing his heart out.

I knelt down beside the bed and took him, covers and all, into my arms and began to cry with him. Finally, I pulled the covers off him and gathered him in my arms and said, "The Lord told me what happened yesterday on the job." *Thank God, He did. You see, when God moves in a supernatural way, it convinces people of His love and mercy for them.*

I said, "Brother Sam, we're not going to let the devil have you." He sobbed and said, "Brother Hagin, I've always been a hot-tempered man. Something went wrong on the job yesterday, and I let my temper get away from me. The men said I cursed, and they know I got saved two weeks ago. To tell you the truth, I got so angry, I don't know what I did. I'm not going back to church anymore. The Lord doesn't love me."

I said, "The Lord doesn't love the fact that you cursed. But He still loves you. And we're not going to let the devil have you." Then he said, "Oh, my back is hurting so badly, I couldn't get out of bed this morning."

He was just a baby, two weeks old. Spiritually he hadn't learned to walk yet. Babies can't walk. I laid my hand on his back and said, "Dear Lord, I know You love Sam. Just prove your love to him right now." Sam jumped. "It's all gone! It's all gone! The Lord does love me, doesn't He?"

c.   We should look to God for supernatural equipment in ministry. He has furnished it.

1. Paul wrote a letter to the Church at Corinth and said, "... *covet earnestly the best gifts* ..." (1 Cor. 12:31). He also said, "... *desire spiritual gifts* ..." (1 Cor. 14:1).

   He did not write John Smith at the Church of Corinth, saying, "John, I want you to covet the best gifts."

2. He told the whole Church, "covet spiritual gifts." *The Amplified Bible* says, "earnestly desire" spiritual gifts (1 Cor. 14:1).

   If a body of people will covet and earnestly desire the supernatural demonstration of God, then as the Holy Spirit wills, He will manifest Himself through different people in the local body, particularly through this pastoral office.

d. Some seminaries teach psychology. Psychology is the study of the mind and behavior of man. But man is more than just *mind* (2 Thess. 5:23).

   And in a moment of time, like a flash, I've seen the Spirit of God deal with matters by the gifts of the Spirit that psychology or psychiatry couldn't solve in months or years or ever, for that matter.

e. The Spirit of God has equipped the New Testament Church with supernatural ability, supernatural power, and supernatural gifts. He has called men and women to the ministry, and He equips them to stand in their offices supernaturally.

f. Expect God to help you. Train your spirit to be sensitive to the Holy Spirit. Expect the Holy Spirit to manifest Himself through you and to use you for His glory. Listen to Him. Yield to Him.

M. *The most outstanding characteristic of a pastor is a shepherd's heart.*

1. The shepherd's heart is a gift from God to the local body.

    a. Thank God for those who have a shepherd's heart and who love people. They are loyal to the flock, sometimes even at the expense of depriving themselves of some of the simple pleasures of life in order to serve their congregations.

    b. It takes the shepherd's heart to see after baby Christians — to love and nurture them, to nourish them with the Word, and to bear with them when they first start trying to walk spiritually.

    c. In more than 40 years of field ministry, how my heart has gone out to people! I've seen the great need of pastors with a true shepherd's heart. I've preached in more than one church where I thought, *Dear Lord, that man is not a pastor. How these people need a pastor!*

       How they needed someone who would really minister to them and love them! My own heart has ached for them.

       I'd say, "O God, I just wish You would let me pastor them. Just let me put my arms around all of them and love them."

    d. People understand love. Even an old cur dog understands love. People may not understand tongues, but they understand love. And you have to prove to people that you love them. Pastors must love people.

2. The greatest example of a shepherd is the Lord Jesus Christ Himself. Remember what He said: *"I am the good shepherd: the good shepherd giveth his life for the sheep"* (John 10:11).

   The good shepherd gives his life for the sheep.

The Teacher

EPHESIANS 4:11
11 And he gave some, apostles; and some, prophets; and some, evangelists; and some, pastors and TEACHERS.

1 CORINTHIANS 12:28,29
28 And God hath set some in the church, first apostles, secondarily prophets, THIRDLY TEACHERS, after that miracles, then gifts of healings, helps, governments, diversities of tongues.
29 Are all apostles? are all prophets? ARE ALL TEACHERS? . . .

ROMANS 12:4-8
4 For as we have many members in one body, and all members have not the same OFFICE:
5 So we, being many, are one body in Christ, and every one members one of another.
6 Having then gifts differing according to the grace that is given to us, whether prophecy, LET US PROPHESY according to the proportion of faith;
7 Or ministry, LET US WAIT on our ministering: or HE THAT TEACHETH, ON TEACHING.
8 Or he that exhorteth, on exhortation: he that giveth, let him do it with simplicity; he that ruleth, with diligence; he that sheweth mercy, with cheerfulness.

A. Teachers and teaching hold a well-defined and important place in the New Testament.

B. The teacher is the only one mentioned by name in all three lists of ministry.

C. One can stand in the office of pastor and teacher, or prophet and teacher, or evangelist and teacher, and so forth. In other words, one can stand in more than one office. We separate the offices to define them.

   1. Acts 13:1 names five men who were either prophets or teachers, or prophets and teachers.

      ACTS 13:1
      1 Now there were in the church that was at Antioch CERTAIN PROPHETS AND TEACHERS; as Barnabas, and Simeon that was called Niger, and Lucius of Cyrene, and Manaen. . . .

      a. Barnabas was a teacher (Acts 11:22-26; 13:1).

      b. Paul was a prophet and a teacher (Gal. 1:12; Eph. 3:3; 1 Tim. 2:7).

      c. Both became apostles (Acts 14:14).

D. One who is a teacher but not a pastor (that is, he does not have the oversight of a flock) many times has a roving ministry among the churches.

   1. If one is a pastor and a teacher (and often this is the case), he would not necessarily have a roving ministry, although he may go out at times to teach.

E. *The teaching gift is a divine gift.*

   God is talking about an *office* when He talks about the teacher (Rom. 12:4).

He is talking about men or women who are called by God and are set by the Spirit of God to stand in that office to teach by supernatural ability.

1. We have left the impression that Sunday School teachers are the gift He is talking about.

    a. The Early Church did not have Sunday School. Sunday School didn't start until the 18th Century.

    b. Naturally, a person who knows the Bible can teach what he knows. Any Christian can and should share with others what they know by teaching and helping them. *But this is not that teaching gift God is talking about in these passages where the teaching ministry gift is listed.*

F. *The teaching ministry requires a divine gift.*

1. *Personal experience.* I had been preaching for a good many years. I was not a teacher. I was strictly a preacher. All I had learned was what we call "the evangelistic message" or the salvation message in its simplest form. I didn't even have a pastoral message for the saints. But, oh, how I loved to preach! And if I can say it humbly, I could preach up a storm. The power would fall on us while I was preaching and great things would happen. I would preach so hard and fast people would say, "Slow down. We don't get half of what you're saying." It just flowed out of me like a river. And really — in my immaturity and lack of spiritual growth — I didn't think you could be anointed unless you were preaching like a buzz saw, waving your arms like a windmill, and spitting cotton.

    I did not like to teach. Although I taught the adult Sunday School class in the same church I pastored, I was never so glad of anything as when that teaching class was over on Sunday morning so I could get back to preaching. I detested teaching so much that often I wouldn't even look at the teaching quarterly until 45 minutes before time to start.

I did a fairly thorough job. The class grew and the people were blessed. But I was so glad when it was over each Sunday. I'd breathe a sigh of relief and say, "Thank God that's over for another week." I did not like to teach. That was not a part of me.

But one Thursday afternoon in June 1943, in the parsonage of that church, as I walked across the living room toward the bedroom at 3 o'clock in the afternoon, *suddenly something dropped down inside me.*

The best way I know to explain it is that it was like a coin dropping into a pay telephone. You can hear a coin drop into the phone. I could almost hear it. And I knew I could "feel" it. Something dropped down inside me in my spirit. It came from Heaven.

I stopped and stood still because the Spirit of God had come upon me. And without thinking, these words came out of my mouth, "Now I can teach." I recognized what it was by the Spirit of God. *It was a divine endowment* and a divine enablement to teach.

I like to prove things out — that's just part of my nature. So I started on Wednesday afternoons exercising the gift of teaching. I didn't exercise it at any other time. Six or eight women met regularly at 2:30 on Wednesday afternoons for a time of prayer. They were really the prayer warriors in the church who carried the burden for many others. We did continue to pray, but I also began to teach on various subjects, exercising this teaching gift.

I never made any public announcement about those Wednesday afternoon services. People knew the ladies came and prayed, but it was never mentioned from the pulpit that I had started teaching. These women, however, told their husbands what was happening. Some of these husbands began to take off from their jobs and came on Wednesday afternoons. They told others. The crowd grew. Soon the building was filled up at 2:30 on Wednesday afternoons! That was unheard of in those days.

It amazed me. I would literally shake my head in amazement sometimes because a greater anointing would come upon me as I stood there calmly teaching, than when I would preach at the top of my voice and wave my arms like a windmill.

G.   *A teacher is not a teacher merely by virtue of natural ability or a natural inclination to teach.*

    1.   Natural ability and inclination may provide a background for this gift — but the teaching gift is not a natural gift; it is a divine endowment to teach God's Word.

        a.   I've known people who were school teachers before they were born again. They were saved and filled with the Spirit and became able teachers in Bible classes in church. And it was right for them to do so. But this is not the ministry gift of teaching in demonstration.

H.   No teaching ministry in the power of the Holy Spirit is dry! It will convey rivers of living water.

    1.   Paul described the teaching ministry as watering.

> **1 CORINTHIANS 3:6-9**
> **6 I have planted, APOLLOS WATERED; but God gave the increase.**
> **7 So then neither is he that planteth any thing, NEITHER HE THAT WATERETH; but God that giveth the increase.**
> **8 Now he that planteth AND HE THAT WATERETH are one: and every man shall receive his own reward according to his own labour.**
> **9 For we are labourers together with God: YE ARE GOD'S HUSBANDRY** [garden]. . . .

        a.   A minister of the gospel was ministering in an area of the United States well known for greenhouses and nurseries. One elderly gentleman in the church invited the visiting minister to see the greenhouse where he tended the plants. The minister was amazed at what he saw. He said, "I've never seen such luxurious growth."

Two years later the minister was back in the area. He asked to be taken to the greenhouse again. "The minute I walked inside," he said, "I could tell something was wrong." It was the same greenhouse. They had the same kinds of plants. But they just were not as luxurious. There was a remarkable difference.

"It's not like it was two years ago. What happened?" he asked the attendants. They knew what was wrong. They answered, "The older gentleman who cared for the plants and watered them correctly died. We have someone else doing it now."

b. Many a work of God has been ruined because the watering process wasn't there to encourage people to cleave to the Lord and to become a beautiful garden for God.

c. *When the watering process — that is, the teaching of the Word of God — is carried out by a spiritual gift because one is called and endowed to teach, it leaves people refreshed and revived, just as watering a plant leaves it revived and fresh.*

d. If teaching does not leave people refreshed, it simply is not being executed and carried out in the power of the Holy Spirit.

2. Apollos was a teacher. It was said of him, "he helped them much."

ACTS 18:27
27 And when he was disposed to pass into Achaia, the brethren wrote, exhorting the disciples to receive him: who, when he was come, HELPED THEM MUCH WHICH HAD BELIEVED THROUGH GRACE.

a. These people had already believed through grace — they were already saved.

b. In exercising this teaching gift, Apollos helped them much.

I. Divisions can be caused by unbelief and hardness of heart, even when teaching is in the power of the Spirit based on the Word of God.

1. Under the ministry of Jesus this happened. Some would not accept His teaching. On one occasion the Bible says, *"From that time many of his disciples went back, and walked no more with him"* (John 6:66).

J. A true teacher of the gospel of peace will never teach doctrinal error which will split the Body of Christ. He will not cause division by what he teaches.

K. On the other hand, we cannot compromise on the fundamental principles of the doctrine of Christ.

1. In Hebrews 6:1,2, we have the fundamental principles of the doctrine of Christ. These things are fundamental and cannot be compromised:

a. Repentance from dead works.

b. Faith toward God.

c. The doctrine of baptisms.

d. Laying on of hands.

e. Resurrection of the dead.

f. Eternal judgment.

L. Other things are not fundamental and you do not want to create division.

M.   Use wisdom.

    1.   Don't just go out and try to convert everyone overnight to the faith message. Some will never get it. Just love them anyhow, because the Lord loves them, and He is not going to forsake them.

N.   The work of a teacher is to build up — not tear down.

    1.   Christ gave teachers for the edifying and building up of the Body of Christ (Eph. 4:11,12).

    2.   To edify means "to build up." He did not give teachers to divide the Body.

        a.   Sometimes it is wisdom to avoid teaching certain truths for a period of time if those truths are causing confusion and division.

        b.   Paul himself said to the Church at Corinth and to the Hebrew Christians, in effect, "There are some things I would like to tell you, but you couldn't bear it, so I'm not going to tell you now" (1 Cor. 3:1,2; Heb. 5:11-14).

            He still loved them. But they were babies. They needed to grow up spiritually.

O.   Teachers should be always ready and open to receive fresh glimpses of truth from the Word of God.

    1.   Revelation marks a teacher's ministry.

    2.   Be teachable. I would not listen to a teacher who was not willing to be taught.

    3.   Keep a humbleness of spirit and a humbleness of mind.

    4.   Keep an open mind and be always ready to learn.

Whom God Calls,
He Equips

A.   *The ministry gifts are people* — people who are called of God to the full-
time ministry.

    1.   Philip is called an evangelist.

    2.   Peter is called an apostle.

    3.   Paul is called a prophet and a teacher first, and later on an apos-
tle.

    4.   Other people in the New Testament are called ministry gifts.

B.   Those people (ministry gifts) whom God calls, *He equips with spiritual
gifts.*

    1.   These ministries are not based on *natural* gifts, but on spiritual
gifts — *supernatural* gifts.

        a.   Not realizing this, results in the Church and the ministry
getting away from the supernatural into the natural.

    2.   When a person is born again, God has in mind what He called that

person to do. With the new birth, one is equipped with certain spiritual talents to equip him to stand wherever he is set in the Body of Christ.

3. Being filled with the Holy Spirit enhances that.

Personal experience: I preached two or three years without the baptism of the Holy Spirit, yet the same anointing came on me to preach then as it does now.

4. *God equips people with the spiritual gifts necessary to stand in the office He calls them to.*

    a. Laymen can have spiritual gifts operating through them. But ministers will be equipped to minister regularly with those gifts necessary to stand in the office they are called to.

    b. The same spiritual gifts operating through the ministerial level will carry a greater anointing than it does operating occasionally in a layman's life.

    Example: Tongues and interpretation or prophecy operating through the ministerial level carry a greater anointing than when operating through the laymen level.

5. Education is good — but we need more than education. Ambition, if it is legitimate (seeking that for which Christ has apprehended) is good — but we need more than ambition. *We need a ministry equipped with supernatural gifts.*

C. The ministry gifts consist *not in name, but in power.*

1. It is easy to call yourself something, but that doesn't make you that.

You can sit in a garage and call yourself a car, but that doesn't make you one.

2. You can call yourself a pastor, but that doesn't make you one.

    You can call yourself an apostle, but that doesn't make you one.

    The proof of the pudding is in the eating. In other words, the ministry to which you are called will be evident in your life. You will have the divine enablement or endowment to stand in the office to which you are called.

D. All the work of the ministry comes under the *lordship* of Jesus Christ.

    1. Jesus Christ is the Head of His body, the Church. The Head and the body are one; therefore, Jesus directs all operations of His body from the right hand of God the Father.

        MARK 16:20
        20 And they went forth, and preached every where, THE LORD WORKING WITH THEM, AND CONFIRMING THE WORD with signs following....

        a. Notice it was their Lord working with these early disciples.

        b. It was as their Lord and not merely as their Helper that Jesus worked with the disciples. Although He is our Helper, through the Holy Ghost, He is also our Lord.

    2. The *Lord Jesus Christ* is the Head of the Church.

        a. He is the One who gave.

        b. He is the One who calls.

        c. He is the One who equips.

        d. Let *Him* do it.

Faithfulness to The Call

Introduction: Some people in the ministry were either never called, or they are hopelessly unfaithful. Why? Because God didn't plan any spiritual failures. Whether we are individual members of Christ, or we are called to be a ministry gift, He did not give some to be failures and some to succeed. No, He planned that all would succeed. Therefore, some ministers are either hopelessly unfaithful, or they were never called. You see, you have to apply yourself to the calling of God upon your life. Ministries don't just happen any more than marriages just happen. You have to work at a marriage, just as you do the ministry.

A. *Study.* Preparation time is never lost time.

> **2 TIMOTHY 2:15**
> **15 Study to shew thyself approved unto God, a workman that needeth not to be ashamed, rightly dividing the word of truth.**

B. *Dedicate.* Along with the call goes a dedication.

C. *Consecrate.* Along with the call goes a consecration.

D. *Submit to the will of God.* Along with the call goes a submission to the will of God.

Comments: When you're first beginning in the ministry, you don't start out on top. Even in climbing a ladder, no one starts out on the top rung. They start on the bottom rung and climb up. You have to do that in ministry. And sometimes the first years of ministry are a great sacrifice. But if you know the call is there, you will stay in there no matter what it may cost you.

You have to make this kind of a consecration to God: *Go under or over, sink or swim, live or die, I'm staying with it because God called me.*

Because you are going out by faith, you know it's not going to wind up that way — but it will look that way sometimes. It will look as if you are going to do all of them — go under, sink, and die.

But if you will stay faithful at those times when it looks as if you're going under, when it looks as if you're sinking, when it looks as if you're dying — YOU WILL GO OVER BECAUSE YOU ARE CALLED OF GOD!!!

Example: Many years ago a man and his wife and two small children went on the foreign mission field. They were Full Gospel missionaries before there were any organized Full Gospel churches. He told me that the first six months it looked as though he and his wife and both children were going to starve to death. "It would have been easy to come home," he said. "But we stayed put because we knew God had called us. And we knew what God's Word said. I made this dedication to God. 'We will stay with it even if all four of us die.'"

They didn't die. Before the year was out they were flourishing financially.

But if they had not been faithful, it would not have happened. Had they griped and complained and said, "I don't know why this happened to us. If God called us, why doesn't He provide for us?" God would not have been able to do what He wanted to do for them, and they would have been failures.

E.   *Be a person of integrity.*

1.   Psalm 15:4 gives one of the characteristics of a spiritual pilgrim as, "*. . . He that sweareth to his own hurt, and changeth not.*"

2. People who have the call of God on their lives and who are also people of integrity — honest and sincere — will stay hooked up with God.

F. *Develop. Mature. Grow.*

   1. Ministries are developed. If you are called to the ministry, take time to develop the ministerial gift.

   2. It takes time for people to become equipped to do what God has for them to do. They must not only be equipped spiritually; they must mature naturally and spiritually.

   3. Usually people start out in a different area of ministry from what God called them to.

      a. Saul (Paul) is named as one of the five prophets and/or teachers in Acts 13. Later the New Testament calls him an apostle. But he didn't start out with an apostle's ministry. He started out as a preacher (Gal. 1:11,15,16,23).

      b. Philip started out in the ministry of helps (Acts 6:1-6). He was faithful in that office. Later he was moved to the office of the evangelist (Acts 8:5-7; 21:8).

      c. If God called you to pastor, you will not begin pastoring a church of 2,000. You would not know how to handle the job. You may start with a small flock, or as an assistant, or associate pastor, youth pastor, and so forth.

      d. God may have called you to be an evangelist. You may eventually preach to 5,000. But you won't start out preaching to 5,000. You may start out by preaching to five.

      e. Do not despise the day of small things (Zech. 4:10).

4. Take time to wait and see what God wants you to do. Let God make you the minister He wants you to be.

    a. Don't say, "I choose this office." You cannot choose. God alone sets people in ministry gift offices.

    b. Don't try to be like someone else. Just be yourself. Take the truth of God's Word that is revealed to you and let God use your personality to inject it. Then it becomes your message.

    c. Don't just say, "I'm a teacher." Stop and wait and find out whether that is what you are or not.

    d. Just because you had one revelation or have given a few words of prophecy, don't say, "I'm a prophet."

        From all probability you are not.

        Even if your call were as a prophet, you couldn't enter that office right away. You wouldn't be capable.

        God will not violate His own rules. His Word says not to put a novice in the office of deacon (1 Tim. 3:6). God will not put an immature Christian or an immature preacher into the office of prophet.

    e. Get some spiritual growth and development under your belt before you try to ascertain and advertise what office you are in.

    f. If God called you and set you in an office, you won't have to advertise it, anyway. People will find out eventually. If they do not, it is not your ministry.

    g. If the ministry is there in embryo stage, it will develop as you are faithful.

    h. You must first determine whether or not the call of God is there. Then be faithful to work for God wherever you are. (To

5. Don't be a "know-it-all."

    a. I'm still learning, aren't you? Wouldn't it be terrible if all you ever knew in life is what you know right now?

    b. God has brought me revelation truth from the Word of God, and when it came, I felt so foolish I said to my wife, "It's a wonder to me that I've been so stupid."

    c. The more you learn, the less you see you know.

    d. A great and wise man of God, W. I. Evans, used to say, "We know so little, because the more we learn, the less we see we know."

P. Here is a revelation the Lord brought to me. In fact, Jesus said it to me in a vision when He appeared to me in February 1959 and talked to me about what my offices were (prophet and teacher). It astounded me. Yet He proved it to me by the Word.

First, He told me that I had gotten my ministry out of order by putting the teaching ministry first. I had to put the prophet's ministry first.

Then He explained that in all three instances in the Word where the ministries of the prophet and teacher are mentioned, the prophet's ministry is always mentioned first.

1. *"And God hath set some in the church, first apostles, secondarily PROPHETS, thirdly TEACHERS, after that miracles, then gifts of healings, helps, governments, diversities of tongues"* (1 Cor. 12:28).

2. *". . . he gave some, apostles; and some, PROPHETS; and some, evangelists; and some, pastors and TEACHERS"* (Eph. 4:11).

3. *"Now there were in the church that was at Antioch certain PROPHETS and TEACHERS; as Barnabas, and Simeon that was called Niger, and Lucius of Cyrene, and Manaen, which had been brought up with Herod the tetrarch, and Saul"* (Acts 13:1).

Jesus went on to say, "The teaching office *to the Church* is more important than working of miracles or gifts of healings."

Then Jesus explained what He meant by that. The teacher is more important to the Church — to those who are already saved. You see, working of miracles or gifts of healings often indicate the evangelist's office, which is not *to the Church*, but to *the sinner*.

But the teaching ministry is more necessary *to the Church* because the saints need to be taught, edified, and matured by the teaching of the Word. Besides, working of miracles and gifts of healings (or any spiritual gift) will never establish a Christian in faith. But teaching the Word will.

Some feel the teaching ministry gift is an inferior calling. It is not. Remember, we all need one another.

Variety of
Ministry Gifts

EPHESIANS 4:8,11,12
8   Wherefore he saith, When he ascended up on high, he led captivity captive, and gave gifts unto men. . . .
11 And he gave some, APOSTLES; and some, PROPHETS; and some, EVANGELISTS; and some, PASTORS and TEACHERS;
12 For the perfecting of the saints, for the work of the ministry, for the edifying of the body of Christ.

1 CORINTHIANS 12:28-30
28 And God hath set some in the church, first APOSTLES, secondarily PROPHETS, thirdly TEACHERS, after that MIRACLES, then GIFTS OF HEALINGS, HELPS, GOV-ERNMENTS, DIVERSITIES OF TONGUES.
29 Are all apostles? are all prophets? are all teachers? are all workers of miracles?
30 Have all the gifts of healing? do all speak with tongues? do all interpret?

ROMANS 12:4-8
4   For as we have many members in one body, and all members have not the same office:
5   So we, being many, are one body in Christ, and every one members one of another.

6 Having then gifts differing according to the grace that is given to us, whether PROPHECY, let us prophesy according to the proportion of faith;
7 Or MINISTRY, let us wait on our ministering: or he that TEACHETH, on teaching;
8 Or he that EXHORTETH, on exhortation: he that GIVETH, let him do it with simplicity; he that RULETH, with diligence; he that sheweth MERCY, with cheerfulness.

A. Ephesians 4:11 lists the fivefold ministry gifts — those who are preachers and/or teachers of the Word of God.

B. The two other lists of ministries also contain those called as supportive to the fivefold ministry offices and adds further definition of some of the fivefold offices.

C. Taken together, these three passages reveal the fullest measure of the breadth of ministry Christ gave to the Church in ministry gifts.

   1. Four Greek words are translated "gifts" in the New Testament.

   2. The one translated "gifts" in relation to ministry gifts means *a spiritual endowment.*

      a. *A ministry office is a spiritual endowment from God.*

      b. *If God calls you to an office, He endows you with what it takes to fill that office.*

D. In the catalog of ministry in Romans 12:6-8:

   1. We immediately recognized *the prophet* (v. 6).

   2. We immediately recognize *the teacher* (v. 7).

   3. "He that *ruleth*" is probably synonymous with *the pastor* (v. 8).

      a. That's because the pastor is the one who oversees and governs the local body.

4. *In addition* we find *ministers* (v. 7).

5. *Exhorters* (v. 8).

6. *Givers* (v. 8).

7. *Those who show mercy* (v. 8).

E. In the catalog of ministry in First Corinthians 12:28:

1. We find *apostles* (v. 28).

2. *Prophets* (v. 28).

3. *Teachers* (v. 28).

4. *Miracles* and *gifts of healings* are regarded as a distinct ministry (v. 28).

   a. We have already seen that these gifts have a special place in the ministry of an evangelist (Acts 8:5-7,13).

   b. Miracles and gifts of healings are by no means confined to the evangelist's office alone.

5. *Helps* (v. 28).

   a. We find no adequate parallel for the ministry of helps in Ephesians 4:11.

   b. We believe its parallel is supplied in Romans 12 as we will see later.

6. *Governments* (v. 28).

   a. Probably the equivalent of pastors in Ephesians 4:11.

   b. Probably the equivalent of "he that ruleth" in Romans 12.

7. *Diversities of tongues* (vv. 28,30).

    a.   This is a definite ministry set by God in the Church.

    b.   According to First Corinthians 14:5, this would correspond closely to the ministry of the prophet when it is accompanied with the gift of interpretation.

F.   The divine source is emphasized in all three ministry lists.

G.   Some of these gifts — particularly those listed in Romans 12 — may appear to be lacking in the supernatural element. Yet *all come from a supernatural source, given by the same Spirit, and given by grace.*

    1.   The supernatural endowment in the offices such as helps and governments may not be as spectacular as it is in some of the other offices, but it is just as supernatural.

The Office
Of Helps

1 CORINTHIANS 12:28
28 And God hath set some in the church, first apostles, secondarily prophets, thirdly teachers, after that miracles, then gifts of healings, HELPS, governments, diversities of tongues.

A. Right in the middle of this ministry gift list — right in the midst of apostles, prophets, teachers, evangelists, and pastors — we find *the ministry of helps.*

    1. As we have said, the Church world has been hurt by recognizing only two or three ministry gifts.

        a. When I first started out in ministry, all we recognized were evangelists and pastors.

        b. I automatically thought if God didn't call me to pastor, then He had to be calling me as an evangelist. I was in the ministry many years before I realized my calling was neither pastor nor evangelist.

    2. Your calling might be to the ministry of helps.

a. If that is true, then to try to get into another office is really intruding, and trouble will result.

   1. I believe unknowingly many people who were called to the ministry of helps and would have been a great blessing to the Church if they had been privileged to stand in that office, have failed in their ministry because they did not stand in the helps ministry as they should have.

   2. Oftentimes, they have thought, *I sense the call to the ministry. Therefore I must be a pastor or an evangelist.* They try to function in one of those offices and never really succeed because they aren't called to those offices.

B. The actual Greek word translated "helps" occurs only in First Corinthians 12:28.

C. The Greek lexicon gives its meaning as *a helper or a reliever.*

   1. You can see what benefit and assistance this ministry can provide, especially as a supportive role to the fivefold ministry gifts.

   2. Probably the best explanation of the helps ministry is found in the related list in Romans 12:8: "those who show mercy."

      a. According to *Vine's Expository Dictionary of New Testament Words,* the ministry of helps is "one of the ministrations in the local church, by way of rendering assistance, perhaps especially of help ministered to the weak and needy."[1]

      b. *The Amplified Bible* translates Romans 12:8: ". . . he who does acts of mercy, with genuine cheerfulness and joyful eagerness."

      c. A. S. Way renders the passage, "If you come with sympathy to sorrow, bring God's sunlight in your face."

D. The one who helps must have the real equipment of divine grace and power.

E. Romans 12:7 says, *"Or ministry, let us wait on our ministering. . . ."*

1. In the New Testament, the word translated "minister" is used generally to refer to all those who minister in sacred things, including the apostles.

    a. First of all, in Romans 12:7 the word "ministry" can be used as all-inclusive instruction that whatever ministry you are in, "let him that ministers wait on his ministry."

        1. What does that mean? That means to be successful and to be able to minister effectively, you will have to take time to prepare yourself in the Word and to wait before God in prayer.

2. However, as the word "ministry," is used in Romans 12:7, it also seems to indicate a distinctive ministry from the others mentioned. It is probably referring to the ministry of a *deacon* (Acts 6:1-6).

    a. This word "deacon" is used in Philippians 1:1 and First Timothy 3:8-13.

    b. It is used of Phebe in Romans 16:1 and is translated "servant."

    c. The deacon's ministry in the early days of the Church was especially connected with having charge of the alms of the assembly and being an overseer of the poor and the sick.

    d. The deacon's ministry is a divine gift from Jesus Christ, the Head of the Church. It requires more than mere natural ability to effectively fulfill this ministry, just as it does any other ministry.

3. Acts 6:1-6 describes the appointing of seven men to serve as deacons in the ministry of helps.

ACTS 6:1-6

1 And in those days, when the number of the disciples was multiplied, there arose a murmuring of the Grecians against the Hebrews, because their widows were neglected in the daily ministration.

2 Then the twelve called the multitude of the disciples unto them, and said, It is not reason that we should leave the word of God, and serve tables.

3 Wherefore, brethren, look ye out among you seven men of honest report, full of the Holy Ghost and wisdom, whom we may appoint over this business.

4 But we will give ourselves continually to prayer, and to the ministry of the word.

5 And the saying pleased the whole multitude: and they chose STEPHEN, a man full of faith and of the Holy Ghost, and PHILIP, and Prochorus, and Nicanor, and Timon, and Parmenas, and Nicolas a proselyte of Antioch:

6 Whom they set before the apostles: and when they had prayed, they laid their hands on them.

a. Philip started out here in the ministry of helps (v. 5). He was helping the apostles wait on tables so they could pray and give themselves to prayer and the ministry of the Word. As Philip proved himself faithful, God moved him on to become an evangelist (Acts 21:8).

b. Stephen also started out in the ministry of helps. God used him in a mighty way (Acts 6:8).

c. The other five men are mentioned nowhere else. Evidently they continued in the ministry of helps.

d. Although the names of these five men are not mentioned elsewhere in the New Testament, if they were faithful in their office, they will receive as great a reward as Philip and Stephen.

4. Paul wrote concerning two that helped him: *"Greet Priscilla and Aquilla my helpers in Christ Jesus: Who have for my life laid down their own necks: unto whom not only I give thanks, but also all the churches of the Gentiles"* (Rom. 16:3,4).

5. He also wrote, *"Greet Mary, who bestowed much labour on us"* (Rom. 16:6).

6. A host of others are named in the New Testament who fulfilled the helps ministry.

F. *The ministry of music.* The ministry of music functions as a *helps* ministry, supportive to the fivefold ministry.

1. What a help! What an aid! What an assist is the ministry of music. The ministry of music is not a distinct *office*; it is the *ministry of helps* in operation.

2. It is an *anointed* ministry.

    a. It is not just something someone does because they are talented.

    b. God can use *talent* if people will consecrate their talents to Him.

    c. But it is very distinguishable to those who have the Spirit of God and are sensitive to the things of the Spirit when one is "ministering in song" with the anointing of the Holy Spirit in the ministry of helps, and when one is "just singing."

3. The prophet Elisha called for a *minstrel*. The music ministry can be a great help and assistance to those in the fivefold ministry gifts, particularly the prophet. When the minstrel played his musical instrument, the Holy Spirit came upon the prophet Elisha, and he prophesied.

2 KINGS 3:15,16
15 But now bring me a minstrel. And it came to pass, WHEN THE MINSTREL PLAYED, that THE HAND OF THE LORD CAME UPON HIM.
16 And he said, THUS SAITH THE LORD....

    a. The minstrel's ministry of music was a great help and assistance for the prophet to get into the Spirit.

    b. "The hand of the Lord came upon him" means the Holy Spirit moved upon the prophet. Many times in the Old Testament, the Holy Spirit is referred to as "the hand of the Lord."

    c. Why do you suppose the prophet had the minstrel play? So the minstrel would *hinder* him? No! So the minstrel could *help* the prophet and be an assistance to him.

G. Anything that has to do with helping in the operation of the Church or with ministry could come under the ministry of helps.

    1. People who work in our offices, for instance, are serving in the ministry of helps. I couldn't do it without their help. Thank God for the ministry of helps!

        a. *When the rewards are passed out,* because they were faithful in the ministry of helps, *they will receive just as big a reward as I do.*

        1 SAMUEL 30:24
        24 ... but as his part is that goeth down to the battle, SO SHALL HIS PART BE THAT TARRIETH BY THE STUFF: they shall part [share] alike.

        b. God does not reward according to the office we stand in. *God rewards faithfulness.*

---

[1] W. E. Vine, *Expository Dictionary of New Testament Words* (1940: Fleming H. Revell Company, Old Tappan, New Jersey: 1966), p. 213.

Ministry Tongues And Interpretation

1 CORINTHIANS 12:28-30
28 And God hath set some in the church, first apostles, secondarily prophets, thirdly teachers, after that miracles, then gifts of healings, helps, governments, DIVERSITIES OF TONGUES.
29 Are all apostles? are all prophets? are all teachers? are all workers of miracles?
30 Have all the gifts of healing? DO ALL SPEAK WITH TONGUES? DO ALL INTERPRET?

A. Diversities of tongues (different kinds of tongues) is here regarded as a definite ministry set by God in the Church.

B. Being filled with the Holy Spirit and speaking with other tongues as the Spirit gives utterance in the private prayer life of the believer is not the same as *a ministry of tongues.*

C. What the Word of God is talking about here in First Corinthians 12:28 and 30 is *ministering to others* through tongues and interpretation, as a ministry gift.

1. For instance, the office of the apostle, mentioned first, is not something that blesses and helps the apostle personally. Fulfilling the

office of the apostle, obeying the calling of God to that office, and being spiritually equipped by the Spirit to stand in that office enables the apostle to minister to *others*.

Likewise, the ministry of the prophet is not for the prophet's own personal use. The prophet is equipped by the Spirit of God to enable him or her to minister to others.

It is the same with the ministry of teaching. The teaching gift is not a ministry to teach oneself. Of course, the teacher profits by his own ministry. But his teaching gift is to teach *others* and to bless and minister to *others*.

2. Diversities of tongues is in the same list with apostles, prophets, and teachers. The ministry of *diversity of tongues* is not a ministry for one's own private benefit. The ministry of tongues and interpretation is to be ministered in the public assembly in order to bless and help others. This ministry is not for laymen. It is for those called to the fivefold ministry.

D. When the believer is filled with the Holy Spirit and speaks with other tongues, that is for his own private use and individual edification and prayer life — it is not for others.

1. Speaking in tongues in a person's personal prayer life is primarily a devotional gift.

2. Paul said to the Church at Corinth, *"I thank my God, I speak with tongues more than ye all,"* (1 Cor. 14:18), showing it was primarily a devotional gift to be used in the believer's prayer life in the praise and worship of God.

E. All tongues in essence are the same, but in purpose and use they are different.

F. Only a few of those who are filled with the Spirit and speak with other tongues will be used in the public *ministry of tongues*. Hence Paul asks,

". . . do all speak with tongues? . . ." (v. 30). The answer is obviously no.

1. Some take verse 30 out of context and say, "Speaking in tongues is not for every believer." They try to make the *ministry of tongues* synonymous with the gift of tongues every Spirit-filled believer has in operation in his own private prayer life. And it is not.

2. Taking verse 30 in context, it is clear Paul is talking about the *ministry of tongues* or *diversity of tongues.*

G. Actually, what Paul is talking about in First Corinthians 12:28 when he lists "diversities of tongues" along with the ministry gifts of the apostle, prophet, and teacher, is something separate from the laity "giving an utterance in tongues." It is a ministry gift of tongues and interpretation. There are those called to the fivefold ministry who are called to minister that way, and it most closely approximates the office of the prophet.

Example: The first people I ever saw whom God used along this line were Brother and Sister J. R. Goodwin. For more than 40 years I held meetings in different churches they pastored, and they ministered with me in meetings.

In February 1960, I had just closed a meeting in Beaumont, Texas, before I began a meeting for the Goodwins at the First Assembly of God Church in Pasadena, Texas.

A couple from Beaumont came over to the services in the Goodwins' church in Pasadena one night. The wife had attended all the meetings in Beaumont. The husband had not attended; he was a struggling Christian. The wife had asked me to pray for him at my meetings in Beaumont and had told me some of his problems.

This man came with his wife to the services I was holding for the Goodwins in Pasadena. The Lord had me call them out to come down to the front. I thought He was going to have me minister to them. I knew exactly what He wanted to say to them.

Then as the couple stood there in front of me, like a flash I saw into the spirit realm. I saw them driving back to Beaumont after the service. And I saw the devil attack the wife with doubt, saying, "Well, after all, you told Brother Hagin your problems. He wasn't ministering supernaturally to you because he knew some of those things about you anyway." The devil would try to use that against them to rob them from receiving what God wanted to say to them.

Then the Lord told me, "Have Brother and Sister Goodwin minister to them."

This couple did not know the Goodwins. And the Goodwins did not know them.

Sister Goodwin began to speak with tongues. Brother Goodwin interpreted. They spoke several times back and forth in tongues and interpretation. And ministering supernaturally like that, they drew a better picture of this couple's problem and solution than what I could have done by knowing the situation and ministering to them. I stood there and marveled. It was supernatural! By this ministry gift, diversities of tongues, they told this couple exactly what their problem was, especially his, and exactly what to do about the situation to correct it.

H. As a ministry gift, tongues and interpretation operate together, as we see in this example with Brother and Sister Goodwin.

Exhortation

ROMANS 12:8
8 Or HE THAT EXHORTETH, on EXHORTATION. . . .

A.   This is the only place exhortation is mentioned as a separate and distinct ministry.

    1.   Usually exhortation is regarded as a natural and essential part of almost every other ministry.

B.   The primarily motivation of the exhorter is to bring encouragement either by way of comfort or by stirring up believers.

C.   *There is a distinctive ministry along this line.*

D.   *The exhorter stirs up the lost to be saved.*

    1.   In the days of Sam Jones, the great Methodist evangelist, he would preach a couple of hours then turn the service over to an exhorter to give the altar call. The exhorter would talk sometimes 45 minutes. He would stir up the people, exhorting them to be saved.

2. In my own opinion, many times what we call *evangelists* today are *exhorters*. Their ministry seems to be entirely along the line of stirring up people to be saved.

    a. Those who stand in the office of the evangelist have supernatural gifts (miracles or gifts of healings) following their preaching. This happened in the ministry of our only New Testament example of an evangelist, Philip. A true evangelist has those gifts in operation in his ministry.

    b. I am not belittling the office of the exhorter. It is an office! I am just saying *we have some ministries named incorrectly.*

E. *The exhorter also exhorts Christians with a message of encouragement and comfort.*

The Ministry
Of Giving

ROMANS 12:8
**8 Or he that exhorteth, on exhortation: HE THAT
GIVETH, LET HIM DO IT WITH SIMPLICITY....**

A. *Giving was as much a recognized ministry as teaching or healing in the Early Church.* This is a ministry.

B. We can all enter into the grace of giving, but some have a divine endowment from God to distribute:

    1.   Personal wealth.

    2.   Or administration of united resources.

C. Another translation renders it, "he who has wealth to distribute must do it with a single eye to God's service."

D. Those who have wealth to distribute should distribute correctly, in good places where it is used for God.

    1.   Ministers of the Gospel should take time to teach people about giving:

a.   They should teach congregations about the scriptural ministry of giving.

b.   They should teach those who have wealth to distribute it correctly where it can be used for God's work.

2.   Some scoundrels who call themselves ministers, for instance, raise money for projects which don't exist.

3.   Don't just swallow something because it looks good. *Learn to listen to your spirit.*

4.   Pray and seek God about where to give your money.

E.   Some may sense a call to the ministry, and God has called them to this ministry of giving.

Why should you consider attending
RHEMA
Bible Training Center?

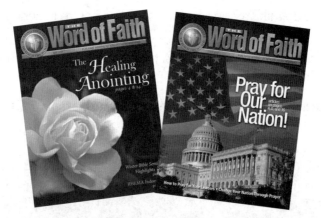